The Open University

Humanities: A Foundation Course　**Units 27–28**

MENDELSSOHN'S REDISCOVERY OF BACH

Prepared by Gerald Hendrie for the Humanities Foundation Course Team

THE OPEN UNIVERSITY PRESS

Fig. 1 *Felix Mendelssohn as a young man.*

Authors:

Section 1 Gerald Hendrie
Section 2 Arthur Marwick
Section 3 Gerald Hendrie
Section 4 Gerald Hendrie
Section 5 Owain Edwards
Section 6 Dinah Barsham

Research Assistants: Richard Middleton
                     Philip Olleson

The Open University Press Walton Hall Bletchley Bucks

First published 1971

Copyright © 1971 The Open University

Designed by The Media Development Group of The Open University

Printed in Great Britain by
OXLEY PRESS LTD.
EDINBURGH AND LONDON

SBN 335 00516 0

Open University courses provide a method of study for independent learners through an
integrated teaching system, including textual material, radio and television programmes
and short residential courses. This text is one of a series that make up the correspondence
element of the Arts Foundation Course.

The Open University's courses represent a new system of university-level education.
Much of the teaching material is still in a developmental state. Courses and course
materials are, therefore, kept continually under revision. It is intended to issue regular
updating notes as and when the need arises, and new editions will be brought out when
necessary.

Further information on Open University courses may be obtained from The Admissions
Office, The Open University, P.O. Box 48, Bletchley, Buckinghamshire.

SECTION 1

CASE STUDY: MARCH 11, 1829: MENDELSSOHN REVIVES BACH'S ST. MATTHEW PASSION.

SOME IMPLICATIONS OF THE REDISCOVERY IN THE NINETEENTH CENTURY OF EARLIER MUSIC

INTRODUCTION

On March 11, 1829, in the hall of the Berlin *Singakademie*[1] the composer Felix Mendelssohn (1809–47) directed a performance of Bach's *St. Matthew Passion*, a setting of the Passion of Jesus Christ according to St. Matthew in one hundred movements, for double choir, double orchestra, boys' choir and soloists. This was exactly a hundred years after its first performance, and was also the first performance since Bach's death in 1750. The hall was filled and a thousand people were turned away. Public demand secured a second performance ten days later, and a third was given shortly after that.

We have chosen this subject as our musical case study in the Humanities Foundation Course for several reasons. First, it acted as a flash-point, creating a new public interest in the work of Johann Sebastian Bach (1685–1750) and of other composers of the past. Second, it shows us the spirit of reverence with which great works of art were beginning to be approached in the early nineteenth century, together with the concept of artist as genius. Third, we can consider the revival in its historical context: the movements in art – Romanticism and Neo-classicism; and the background to the Mendelssohn family's emergence from poverty. In connection with the movements in art just mentioned, I should point out that as has often happened, developments in music lagged behind those in other arts, especially literature. This means that some of the chronology outlined in section 2 is not applicable to music.

The topics and questions that arise from *March 11, 1829*, are many and varied. To start with, the word 'contemporary', so fashionable now, was scarcely meaningful before the middle of the nineteenth century. Today we endeavour to preserve the past: until the nineteenth century, perishable old art was often discarded along with perishable old clothes.

Composers such as Bach and Mozart (1756–91) did not write for posterity. Most likely, they regarded themselves as master-craftsmen who provided a skilled service for which there was plenty of demand. It is unlikely that such men ever had time to philosophize about music and wonder if they were relevant to society. As the deadlines poured in, so their music poured out. But during the nineteenth century a new spirit was abroad. Artists were no longer servants, even if skilled ones; they gradually became emancipated, and started to produce works primarily to please themselves. Not

1 A concert-giving Society founded at Berlin in the early 1790s by Christian Fasch. English translations of *Singakademie* (such as 'Academy of Singing' or 'Vocal Academy') tend to give the wrong impression, so we are retaining the German word.

5

surprisingly, the gulf between artist and society, hitherto generally narrow or seemingly non-existent, began to widen.[1] Rather than attempting to bridge it, the composer of the new generation might think that society was at fault, misunderstanding him because he wrote not for them, but for posterity. The marriage of artist to society, which Bach and Mozart could take for granted, was gradually dissolving. We can detect here a new shift of emphasis, a turning away from the present to either the future or the past. An interest in the future implied a belief in progress – itself very much a nineteenth-century concept – and an interest in the past was again, in all its aspects, a prime manifestation of 'Romanticism'. Yet many Romantics were passionately involved in contemporary movements (which were often endeavouring to bring about some change as a result of a new knowledge of the past or belief in the future), and so again, a paradox is evident.

Notwithstanding a certain professional knowledge of earlier music, notably Bach's, by later composers and a few connoisseurs, nevertheless the public only began to share in this from about the time of Mendelssohn's 'revival'. In fact, Mendelssohn could not have generated such public enthusiasm for a long, difficult, and generally unknown work as Bach's *St. Matthew Passion*, had the intellectual climate of his day not been changing and severing its links with the past.

How did Mendelssohn actually set about reviving and performing the *St. Matthew Passion*? How, for that matter, does anyone rediscover and perform early music? And even possessing a score of Bach's music, how did Mendelssohn know, or how do we know, what Bach meant? There are certain performance practices which are so well known to a composer's contemporaries that he does not bother to notate them. The *St. Matthew Passion* may be full of these, just as modern jazz is. Did Mendelssohn use the same kind of instruments that Bach used, or had they undergone a change during the years following Bach's death? How many singers were involved – as many, fewer, or more than Bach would have used? And was Mendelssohn's *interpretation* of the *St. Matthew Passion* faithful to Bach's intentions (as far as they can be surmised) or was it coloured by a 'Romantic' attitude?

You can see that many of the questions we ask about Mendelssohn's approach to the *St. Matthew Passion* are directly applicable to subsequent performances of any early music. It was problems of this kind that gave rise to the science of musicology in the early years of the nineteenth century. 'Complete Editions' of the works of major composers began to appear, and scholarly textual criticism at last reached the field of music. More than a hundred years later, scholars are still hard at work. Many composers remain without their 'Complete Edition' and others, like Bach and Handel, are in the process of having theirs remade in the light of present-day scholarship.

This leads us to ask further questions. Even if we possess texts based on original sources, is it possible, or even desirable, to endeavour to recreate the original music? Can there ever be, or has there ever been a perfect performance? If so, should we attempt to 'freeze' it into perpetuity by making a gramophone record of it? This raises the whole question of communication in music.

1 See Unit 4, paragraphs 7.15–7.16.

6

These are the kind of topics and questions which arise from *March 11, 1829*. We can summarize them in five General Aims:

1 To define Romanticism and to place Mendelssohn's revival of Bach's *St. Matthew Passion* within the early nineteenth-century context.

2 To define and explain the discipline of musicology and its origins in the early nineteenth century.

3 To introduce you to source material in music.

4 To make you aware of the crucial change from master-craftsman to creative artist or 'genius' that occurred in the early nineteenth century.

5 To consider aspects of technological developments in music and how they may affect musical taste.

This correspondence material is supported by two television programmes and two radio programmes. The first television programme sets the Mendelssohn scene; the second should make you aware of the relevance of musicology to contemporary performance. In the first radio programme the performance-history of Handel's *Messiah*, first performed in 1742, is discussed with particular reference to changes and additions to the score, the use of ever-increasing forces, and subsequent purification. The second radio programme brings an important aspect of our case study up to date: a distinguished younger composer discusses the composition and production of a modern large-scale work.

SECTION 2

THE HISTORICAL CONTEXT

Part 1 ROMANTICISM

In the *Introduction to History* units we discussed both the value and the danger of the historian's attempts to *periodize* and to *establish the historical context*. We can fully appreciate the significance of a concrete event like Mendelssohn's rediscovery and performance of the Bach *St. Matthew Passion* only if we have a knowledge of the historical circumstances in which this event took place. And from the point of view of the historian, one of his basic interests is the study of the relationship between definite events of this sort (which we *know* beyond all doubt took place) and the historical circumstances surrounding the event, which are always much more open to debate and *controversy*. On the other hand if we say that Mendelssohn's action was 'typical of the Romanticism of the period', we have to be very careful that we know what we mean when we talk about *Romanticism*; and also what we mean when we talk of *the period*.

Let us first of all define ROMANTICISM in the most general way, then look more closely at the way in which the use and meaning of the word developed up to the time we are concerned with, the early nineteenth century. Romanticism, in this general sense, implies several, or all, of the following characteristics:

1 A rebelliousness towards established, accepted, modes of thought and ways of doing things.

2 An emphasis on the individual and on originality, rather than on following a definite set of rules.

3 An emphasis on enthusiasm and emotion.

4 An interest in the strange and mysterious.

5 An emphasis on faith, rather than on the dictates of pure reason.

6 An emphasis on the idea of the artist as a genius set apart from the rest of society, rather than as a mere craftsman.

7 Nevertheless, the rebelliousness of the romantic means that he also tends to be involved in, or at least concerned about, the politics of his day.

8 An emphasis on movement and change as against an emphasis on the static, unchanging character of the world.

9 An emphasis on the *different* characteristics of different communities, rather than on the *universal* qualities shared by all of nature and all of mankind: *nationalism* is one form this emphasis can take.

10 A love of exciting, flamboyant, colourful forms, rather than the balanced, restrained ones usually associated with Classicism (which is sometimes seen, not altogether accurately, as representing the opposite of Romanticism).

Fig. 2 *Man and a woman contemplating the moon, by Caspar Friedrich.*

In its modern usage the word *romantic* derives from the mediaeval *romance*, the tales of love and adventure told by the troubadours. It first appears in English in the seventeenth century. Usually among the classical-minded intellectuals of the eighteenth century it was used as a term of abuse, though it could also be used in a more neutral way to describe anything weird and mysterious, particularly paintings which featured strange moonlit effects. At the end of the eighteenth century a group of German writers deliberately took over the word and associated it more positively with the sort of characteristics I have listed above, and, in particular, with their own revolt against the aesthetic standards of the eighteenth century. This notion of a positive Romantic Movement was enthusiastically taken up by many of the most talented young artists and writers throughout Europe. Historically, then, the great period of European Romanticism is the last few decades of the eighteenth century, and the first few decades of the nineteenth century. But Romanticism as an important artistic movement continues until well into the nineteenth century, though in many respects it becomes less dynamic, more genteel and more 'domesticated' as the century wears on.

Now obviously one can see elements of the Romanticism which we have just defined at all periods in human history. There is nothing necessarily new about the romantic elements which some young intellectuals at the beginning of the nineteenth century are stressing. However the critical thing is that these intellectuals see Romanticism as a definite *movement*: that is, they felt themselves to be Romantics, and announced that they were Romantics. This is rather different from the odd individual artist or intellectual in an earlier period showing elements of romanticism. It is not therefore terribly fruitful to try to trace back the origin of Romanticism as some historians have done. Some have traced it back to the Renaissance, some right back to Plato and the ancient Greeks. Let us accept that individuals at all periods in history have shown Romantic characteristics. But what, let me repeat, is of importance here is the *movement* which appears at the end of the eighteenth century and at the beginning of the nineteenth century.

9

Fig. 4 'Domesticated' Romanticism: Biedemeier interior.

Fig. 3 Typical early nineteenth-century Prussian middle-class interior.

However we must not fall into the trap of thinking that everyone in this period was a Romantic, or even that every artist and intellectual was a Romantic. Romanticism is a movement of *ideas*; it is *an attitude of mind* and not a systematic programme. Clearly, within the general movement of Romanticism there can be all sorts of different ideas and interpretations. Even if the majority of articulate artists and intellectuals subscribe to something which they think of as Romanticism, this does not preclude other intellectuals and artists having rather different ideas. More critically one must avoid what I shall call the '*either/or*' interpretation of ideas. This interpretation suggests that first of all in the eighteenth century, as part of the movement of ideas known as 'the Enlightenment', there was something called Classicism or Rationalism, but towards the end of the eighteenth century this gave way to an opposite, Romanticism. Things do not in fact happen this way. You do not have one set of ideas suddenly succeeded by its opposite. And although it is quite correct to think of Romanticism as expressing a rather different set of values from Classicism – Romanticism puts a stress on the particular, the individual, and the open expression in art of strong emotion, whereas Classicism puts an emphasis on harmonious unity and on restraint – in actual fact many artists and writers whom we would probably agree to call Romantics also had within their mental and artistic make-up considerable elements of Classicism (and, of course, it is nonsense to think of eighteenth-century writers as not being emotional). The great German poet, Goethe, who has sometimes been regarded as a leader of the Romantic movement, objected to the term Romantic and continued to stress the value of rationalism and of the classical heritage. Indeed one perfectly reasonable, though perhaps rather limited, analysis of Romanticism would be to see it as a *development from*, rather than a *reaction against*, eighteenth-century Classicism (though, naturally, those who boasted of the label Romantic preferred to stress their rebellious qualities).

However, having given due weight to all the dangers and difficulties inherent in using a blanket label like Romanticism, we must in the end accept it as a real and important historical phenomenon. Remembering one of the points made when we discussed 'Historical Semantics' (Unit 8: *Common Pitfalls in Historical Writing*) let us note in particular that the Romantics themselves, not just later historians,

10

did use the term; they were proud to *call* themselves Romantics. This Romantic Movement is significant both as a *product* of existing historical circumstances, and as an *agent* in creating further historical change.

Let us, then, look at the main historical circumstances giving rise to this movement which we can agree to call Romanticism. First of all what we can call an *internal* cause, something within the realm of ideas, not *directly* related to political, social or economic developments (which we call *external* causes). Even if, in some ways, Romanticism is a development from the eighteenth-century Enlightenment, its first and noisiest spokesmen undoubtedly saw themselves as reacting against what they saw as the played-out, complacent, static, characteristics of Classicism. It is in the nature of artists and poets to innovate, so that even before the appearance of the full Romantic Movement we have what are sometimes called the Pre-Romantics. The young Goethe; Rousseau, in certain aspects of his thought; William Blake and Robert Burns in our own country. These writers, already *before* the upheavals of the French Revolution, show certain characteristics and interests which in the course of time were to be associated with the Romantic movement.

Fig. 5 Blake.

Fig. 6 Burns.

Fig. 7 Goethe.

11

Fig. 8 '14th July 1789 – The Taking of the Bastille.'

However, it probably needed more significant historical circumstances ('external causes') to turn these first stirrings into the deeper and wider phenomenon which Romanticism was to become. First of the two crucial sets of historical circumstances is the great chain of political and social upheavals touched off by the French Revolution. The French Revolution of 1789 showed that the existing political and social structure in France was not eternal. And the French Revolution was followed by a generation of wars which saw the French revolutionary armies, and later the Napoleonic armies, bring down many of the ancient dynasties of Europe. Revolutionary ideas, ideas of dynamic *change*, were spread throughout the length and breadth of Europe. This whole colossal period of upheaval and change gave a tremendous impetus towards the ideas of change which the Romantics were putting forward, and indeed directly inspired many of those ideas. In a strange way, too, Napoleon, the great victorious conqueror, could be seen as the embodiment of the Romantic notion of genius or hero. The other major set of historical circumstances helping to foster the Romantic Movement is the great series of economic changes which in Britain can be given the title, 'the Industrial Revolution'. Even if we do not talk of a French, or a Prussian, or an Austrian industrial revolution, undoubtedly changes in industry and commerce were taking place in the late eighteenth century, which again helped to create a general impression of instability, of novelty and of change, which gave further inspiration to the Romantic theorists in their attack on the established order of the eighteenth century. Most important, a new social class, whose wealth was based on commerce and industry, was coming to the fore, often with tastes and standards different from those of the eighteenth-century aristocracy.

Let us now look at some of the more obvious characteristics manifested by Romanticism as it appeared in the first decades of the nineteenth century. In general the Romantics show a dislike of the established order of things. They may in fact be extreme radicals in politics, strongly critical of the established systems of government. Or they may be strongly conservative, objecting to the excesses of commerce, industrialization and political revolution. Or they may be both radical in some things and conservative in others. But in all cases they want something *different* from what they see around them;

12

Fig. 9 The beginnings of Industrialisation.

Fig. 10 The early Industrial Revolution: sketches of coalmines in Northumberland and Durham.

they will not *accept* that whatever system of society and government happens to exist must automatically be for the best. As we said at the beginning, Romanticism must not be seen as a unified movement. The key point is that all the early Romantics do feel a definite sense of political and social *commitment*, some to revolution, some to conservatism, some to radicalism, some to a democratic brand of nationalism and some to a highly conservative nationalism.

After about 1820 much of this sense of commitment began to weaken: the spirit of revolution seemed to have been defeated with Napoleon in 1815 and on the European continent many of the later Romantics became increasingly identified with the important commercial and industrial classes who were themselves now anxious to avoid any revival of revolutionary sentiment. (Unit 31 will discuss the radical attitudes of such later Romantics in Britain as Carlyle and Dickens.) All Romantics had tended to seek escape from the existing order of society which they disliked, in one or more of three ways: by turning towards a future golden age, by turning away from the works of man towards nature, or by turning towards an alleged golden age in the past. Increasingly after 1820 the Romantics became preoccupied with the past, particularly with the mysterious and colourful, as they saw it, characteristics of the Middle Ages.

These characteristics can be seen in various well-known individual Romantics. Wordsworth, the English poet, was, as a young man, an enthusiastic supporter of the French Revolution, and for most of his life a defender of the English peasants against the encroachments of industrialization, though in later life he became a determined Tory;

13

his poetry shows a sense of mystic communion with nature. Of two other English poets, Shelley was an active radical, and Byron died while fighting on behalf of Greek national freedom from the Turkish empire. In Germany, the critic and leading spokesman for Romanticism, Friedrich Schlegel, and the Romantic poet Eichendorff were deeply interested in both Mediaevalism and German nationalism while the Jewish-born Heine was the eternal rebel against society. Eichendorff, in the post-1820 period became very much an upholder of discreet middle-class taste. The new interest in the past, and the concept of constant *change*, are manifested by Sir Walter Scott (a life-long conservative) and by the German historian, Ranke (a reactionary conservative). The new scientific interest in history, personified by Ranke, is in fact paralleled by a new scientific interest in past music – creating the new subject of musicology.

Fig. 11 Byron.

Fig. 12 Schlegel.

Fig. 13 Schiller.

Fig. 14 Eichendorff.

Fig. 15 Heine.

15

EXERCISE 1

Some of the following extracts either *contain* strong elements of Romanticism or else they *describe* or *refer to* definite Romantic characteristics. Show that you recognize these Romantic elements by placing a tick ($\sqrt{}$) beside the appropriate passage. Place a cross ($\times$) beside the passages which do not show, or refer to any obvious Romantic characteristics. In the box beneath each extract write a brief comment explaining your decision.

A   (extract from a poem)

> For I have learned
> To look on nature, not as in the hour
> Of thoughtless youth; but hearing oftentimes
> The still, sad music of humanity,
> Nor harsh nor grating, though of ample power
> To chasten and subdue. And I have felt
> A presence that disturbs me with the joy
> Of elevated thoughts; a sense sublime
> Of something far more deeply interfused,
> Whose dwelling is the light of setting suns,
> And the round ocean and the living air,
> And the blue sky, and in the mind of man:
> A motion and a spirit, that impels
> All thinking things, all objects of all thought,
> And rolls through all things.

B   (extract from a treatise on painting)

> We cannot . . . recommend an indeterminate manner, or vague ideas of any kind, in a complete and finished picture. This notion, therefore, of leaving anything to the imagination, opposes a very fixed and indispensable rule in our art – that everything shall be carefully and distinctly expressed, as if the painter knew, with correctness and precision, the exact form and character of whatever is introduced into the picture. This is what with us is called Science and Learning; which must not be sacrificed and given up for an uncertain and doubtful beauty.

C   (extract from a novel)

At these words he seized the cold hand of Isabella, who was half
dead with fright and horror. She shrieked, and started from him.
Manfred rose to pursue her; when the moon, which was not up,
and gleamed in at the opposite casement, presented to his sight the
plumes of the fatal helmet, which rose to the height of the windows,
waving backwards and forwards in a tempestuous manner, and
accompanied with a hollow and rustling sound. Isabella, who
gathered courage from her situation, and who dreaded nothing so
much as Manfred's pursuit of his declaration, cried, 'Look! my
lord! See! Heaven itself declares against your impious intentions!'
'Heaven nor hell shall impede my designs!' said Manfred, advancing
again to seize the Princess.

D   (extract from a book by a leading historian of today)

In Germany, the writers of the *Sturm und Drang*, with the initial
support of Schiller and the protection of Goethe, revolted against
every form of authority in an anarchic protest against standards of
taste and behaviour which seemed to them to frustrate all that was
most precious in human individuality. Their world of conflict and
destruction was the antithesis of the Providential or scientific
harmony of the Enlightenment, which had postulated the recon-
ciliation of all differences and the eventual convergence of all honest
reasoning and a potential solution to every problem.

E   (extract from Mazzini's 'Young Italy' programme of 1831)

Young Italy is a brotherhood of Italians who believe in a law of
Progress and *Duty*, and are convinced that Italy is destined to become
one nation – convinced also that she possesses sufficient strength
within herself to become one, and that the ill success of her former
efforts is to be attributed not to the weakness, but to the mis-
direction of the revolutionary elements within her – that the secret
of force lies in constancy and unity of effort. They join this
association in the firm intent of consecrating both thought and
action to the great aim of re-constituting Italy as one independent
sovereign nation of free men and equals.

F   (extract from a book by another historian of today)

Events were no longer submitted to and judged according to
universal and abstract criteria, but considered on their own merits,
and by the light of selfishness, the rational and the contingent, past
and present are indissolubly fused. This bestowed upon the writings
of Michelet, Ranke and Augustin Thierry a wonderful freshness,
but also very often indeed a dangerously misleading seductiveness.
Nations, ages, classes were endowed with a soul, were depicted as
driven by a destiny, as unconsciously realising vast goals across the
ages.

G   (invented extract: what a traveller might have written in 1800)

From a distance the old town of Edinburgh rises proudly above
the new like a noble ship. These magnificent spires and proud
tenements leading in procession down the high ridge presided over
by the majestic castle conceal within their walls the mysteries and
excitements of centuries of human love and human bloodshed.

Fig. 16   The Old Town of Edinburgh.

Fig. 17   Edinburgh's New Town, Adam's classical façade in Charlotte Square.

H   (another invented extract: what a different traveller might
     have written in 1800)

Thank heavens they have built that well-proportioned New Town,
so that all my Scotch friends have escaped from the foul squalor
and smell of the old town of Edinburgh, to a decent, rational and
civilised existence.

I   (extract from a letter from Goethe to Zelter, 9 June 1827)

Taking into account all the things that might weigh against him,
this Leipzig Cantor (Bach) is a phenomenon of God: lucid, but
ultimately not susceptible to elucidation.

J   (extract from a poem)

For Forms of Government let fools contest;
Whate'er is best administer'd is best:
For Modes of Faith, let graceless zealots fight;
. . .
Thus God and Nature link'd the gen'ral frame,
And bade Self-love and Social be the same.

K   (statement by a poet)

The most unfailing herald, companion, and follower of the
awakening of a great people to work a beneficial change in opinions
or institutions is poetry. It is impossible to read the compositions
of the most celebrated writers of the present day without being
startled with the electric life which burns within their words. They
measure the circumference and sound the depths of human nature
with a comprehensive and all-penetrating spirit, and they are
themselves perhaps the most sincerely astonished at its manifesta-
tions: for it is less their spirit than the spirit of the age . . . Poets
are the unacknowledged legislators of the world.

A   This poem shows many of the basic characteristics of Romanticism: nature, nostalgia, mysticism. It is, in fact, a passage from Wordsworth's *Tintern Abbey*.

B   This, taken from Sir Joshua Reynolds' *Discourse* of December, 1778, very much expresses the eighteenth-century rational attitude towards art; in contrast to the Romantic view, it is very strongly opposed to 'leaving anything to the imagination'.

X

C   This is one of the very earliest Romantic novels, the *Castle of Otranto* (1764) written by Horace Walpole. The exaggerated Romantic elements are so obvious as to need no further elaboration here.

√

Fig. 18   Strawberry Hill: eighteenth-century example of Horace Walpole's Gothic imagination.

D   This is a good summary [by Norman Hampson in *The First European Revolution* (Thames and Hudson, 1968)] of the fundamental philosophy of the first German Romantics.

E   This is one of the earliest statements of Italian nationalism; and nationalism, as we have seen, is bound up with the Romantic rejection of the universality of man.

F   Here the writer (J. L. Talmon, in *Romanticism and Revolution*, Thames and Hudson, 1967) is also describing some of the basic elements of Romanticism. It is particularly concerned with the way in which Romanticism affected historical writing, and it shrewdly brings out some of the dangers of the Romantic approach. The first sentence is in fact a very good brief summary of certain essential features of the Romantic attitude.

G   This traveller exhibits the Romantic insistence on seeing mystery and excitement rather than a down-to-earth appreciation of sordidness and nastiness.

H   This traveller, however, prefers to maintain a rational, down-to-earth attitude. The building of the New Town of Edinburgh towards the end of the eighteenth century is usually taken as a good example, in stone and mortar, of the Classical ideas of the eighteenth century.

X

I   There is nothing specifically Romantic in the passage itself so a cross (×) would be entirely appropriate, especially since, by this date, Goethe was strongly hostile to most of the tenets of Romanticism. On the other hand the correspondence material has suggested that there is a link between the revived interest in Bach and the growth of Romanticism, so that you might wish to place a tick (√) in the box. As was suggested in the correspondence material, large issues in history and the humanities often do not resolve themselves into 'either/or' answers.

J   In both style and content these lines of Alexander Pope's form a perfect example of eighteenth-century classical poetry. It is formal and balanced in style and far from seeking change, as the Romantics did, Pope celebrates the happiness of the existing state of affairs.

X

K   The emphasis on the importance of poetry and poets is very much a Romantic one. The words, in fact, are those of the English Romantic poet Shelley.

✓

DISCUSSION

You should have found these exercises fairly straightforward, save, perhaps, for I. If you are at all puzzled you should go back and read the correspondence material again.

(Suggested break)

Fig. 19 Victorian Gothic: St. Pancras Station, London.

Part 2 THE MENDELSSOHN FAMILY IN ITS HISTORICAL CONTEXT

The interests of the historian and the interests of the musicologist come together in a study of the main characteristics of Romanticism, an influence which, after all, pervaded the works of the great musicians of the early nineteenth century. Of some interest, too, to the musicologist (as also to the historian) are the immediate *social* and *economic* circumstances (as distinct from the *intellectual* and *ideological* influence of Romanticism) which may have affected the final shape of a musical composition. We shall turn to this question later. Meantime it is of interest to the historian, though probably not of great interest to the musicologist, to examine some of the longer-term historical developments which are illuminated by a study of Mendelssohn's family background.

The five points which I wish to touch on in this discussion are:

1 The manner in which, from the mid-eighteenth century onwards, greater toleration was extended towards the Jews (first through the influence of 'the Enlightenment', later through the spread of democratic, and revolutionary, ideas).

2 The meaning of religious belief in the eighteenth and in the nineteenth century.

3 The manner in which, in the changing world of the late eighteenth century, it was possible for a family, in two generations, to rise from abject poverty to considerable fortune.

4 The manner in which such a fortune, *not* based on inherited aristocratic position, was becoming increasingly acceptable.

5 The manner in which the spirit of nationalism (itself, as we saw, closely bound up with the spirit of Romanticism) could fire the imagination, and influence the actions, of individuals; and how, in turn, national enthusiasm could further the fortunes of these same individuals.

The story begins in 1743 with the arrival outside the gates of Berlin of the ragged, hunchback Jewish boy, Moses Mendelssohn. Hard work, personal talent, and sheer force of character, enabled Moses Mendelssohn to build up for himself a modest income, and a considerable reputation as a philosophical writer; he was greatly helped by the growing spirit of toleration fostered by the leading writers and thinkers of the eighteenth-century 'Enlightenment' (one such writer was the poet and dramatist, Gotthold Ephraim Lessing, who lived between 1729 and 1781), which helped to combat the virulent anti-semitism which throughout the centuries had condemned Jews to their own inbred ghetto existence. Moses also married Fromet Gugenheim, the daughter of a prosperous Hamburg merchant, and thereby founded the Mendelssohn dynasty. Hamburg was a much freer city than Berlin, capital of Prussia. In those days when there was no unified Germany, only a vast number of small independent states, Hamburg was itself an independent city, headquarters of the Hanseatic traders, the men who dominated the profitable commerce of the entire Baltic area. It was in Hamburg that two of Moses's sons, Abraham and Joseph, established a banking house, just at the time when expanding commerce needed the credit facilities provided by such houses. In the first years of the nineteenth century, Napoleon, now effective ruler of most of Europe as well as of France, endeavoured to starve Britain into submission by closing all continental ports to trade. But, as we noted in the *Introduction to History*, actual concrete reality often differs greatly from the paper decrees of politicians. Since the French representatives in Hamburg were, like many men, corruptible, trade there continued, and the Mendelssohns continued to prosper.

Napoleon, as apostle of the ideas of the French Revolution, had actually aided the cause of the Jews by decreeing their equality throughout the territories he had conquered. But, at the same time, his conquests inspired, among the various peoples of Europe, a sense of *national* identity as part of the resistance to French aggressiveness. Before moving to Hamburg in 1804 Abraham Mendelssohn had lived happily in Paris, but under the pressure of French militarism he was steadily pushed towards identifying himself as an upholder of *German* nationalism, which meant both resistance to France, and support for the idea of all the Germanic states uniting together to form one Germany. Eventually, as Napoleon tightened his blockade, Abraham was forced to flee from Hamburg to Berlin, taking, however, his now considerable wealth with him. Some of this wealth Abraham gave to the cause of the Prussian military effort against Napoleon, and he was thus lauded as a great patriot. In striking contrast to his father's original reception in the Prussian capital, Abraham Mendelssohn was elected to the Berlin Municipal Council.

Felix Mendelssohn, then, was born in 1809 into an extremely prosperous and highly thought-of family which combined commercial status with the intellectual reputation established by the

Fig. 20 Europe in the time of Napoleon.

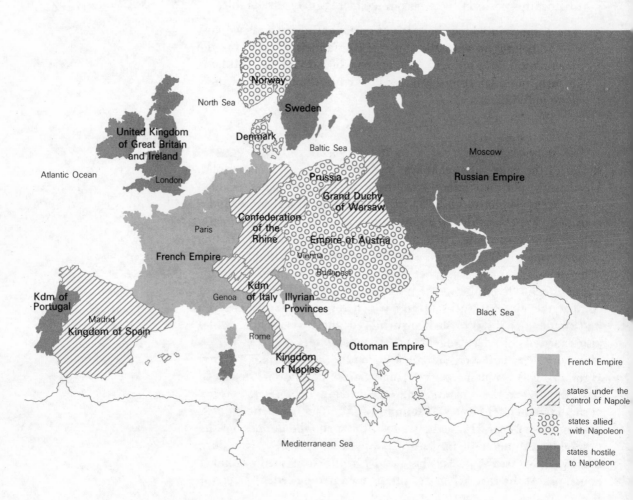

26

philosophical writings of Moses Mendelssohn. When the young Felix showed a musical bent there was no problem at all about sending him to study under the distinguished friend of the family (and of Goethe), Karl Friedrich Zelter, at the Berlin *Singakademie*.

Neither Moses nor Abraham Mendelssohn had any really deep religious convictions; in this sense they shared in the tolerant attitudes of the Enlightenment, and in the general distrust of 'enthusiasm' which characterized it. Abraham had all of his children, including Felix, baptized into the Christian religion and he also tried (unsuccessfully as it proved) to persuade Felix to adopt the non-Jewish name of Bartholdy so that he should become known as Felix Mendelssohn-Bartholdy. Abraham Mendelssohn perhaps shared the sentiments of the Jewish German poet, Heinrich Heine, who described his own baptism as 'a ticket of admission into European culture'. Six years after his son Felix, Abraham did in fact become a Christian; for him this may have been little more than a mere formality. But not for the rising generation. For them the Romantic emphasis on individuality, on emotion, and on spiritual qualities, involved, in many cases, deep religious conviction, and, frequently, a profound interest in the mysteries of mediaeval Christianity.

And that takes us conveniently to the immediate background for the Rediscovery of the Music of Bach. When Johann Sebastian Bach died in 1750 he had the reputation of being the outstanding organist of his day, but his compositions were already thought to be old-fashioned and complicated. They were compared unfavourably with the new, simpler, 'galant' style in which easy melody was combined with a harmonic rather than contrapuntal accompaniment. When, around 1800, some of the Romantics (particularly the German ones) began enthusing over Mediaeval and Renaissance culture, they ran into the problem that most of the music of the period was notated in a way that few could understand. Even when transcribed it would pose performance problems: musical instruments had changed, as had musical forms; furthermore much of this early music is complex and esoteric. In Bach's music, long known and revered by certain professionals, and now beginning to filter through to a wider circle, these Romantics saw something of the mystery of earlier art, combined with a grandeur and even, in a work like the *St. Matthew Passion*, an intensity of expression and sense of the heroic which matched their own aspirations. For the Romantics, Bach represented perfection of faith, perfection of religion, and, therefore, perfection of art. The first biography of Bach was published in 1802 by J. N. Forkel. From then on Bach was much praised, though much less played; one problem being the lack of accessible copies of his works. The young Mendelssohn declared of one Bach chorus that 'if life had taken hope and faith from me, this single chorus would restore all'. But we must not for one moment think of Mendelssohn as being alone in his enthusiasm for Bach. Goethe, and many others, praised Bach for his 'mystical' qualities. The great philosopher of the early nineteenth century, Hegel, spoke of him as 'the master, whose grand, truly Protestant, pithy yet learned genius we have only lately come to value again properly'. And the composer Weber declared that Bach's 'characteristic attitude was, in spite of its rigidity, clearly Romantic and of fundamentally German character . . .'

Karl Zelter, composer, scholar, and Felix Mendelssohn's teacher, admired Bach greatly, and from time to time, performed some of the shorter Bach works at his concerts in the *Singakademie*. He actually had a copy of the *St. Matthew Passion*, but he believed that musically the work was over-complex for contemporary taste, and, as a friend and admirer of Goethe, he thought the words a disgrace to the poetic muse. Yet in 1824 Felix succeeded in getting as a Christmas present from his loving grandmother a copy which she appears to have had transcribed from Zelter's copy. In 1827 Mendelssohn began secretly rehearsing the work with a small choir at his own home. In 1829, thanks partly to the initiative and support of the singer Devrient, who coveted the rôle of Jesus in the *St. Matthew Passion*, Mendelssohn succeeded in obtaining Zelter's permission for a public performance at the *Singakademie*. March 11 was the centenary of the original performance of the work; it was also the centenary of the birth of Moses Mendelssohn. As you have read in the Introduction, the first performance was a sell-out, with one thousand disappointed applicants for tickets. Zelter reported enthusiastically to Goethe on the success of this performance. Hegel attended the second performance held ten days later. A third performance was directed by Zelter himself after Mendelssohn had left for London.

Along with the performance, went *publication* of the work. To the historian *symbols* of the Romantic imagination, performance and publication were together recognized in the world of music as key events in the further development of music.

EXERCISE 2

Listed below are extracts from various primary sources which might be used in studying the life and times of the Mendelssohn family. Comment, in the appropriate box, on how each extract could be related to such a study.

A. (extract from speech by the main character, Nathan, a Jew, in Lessing's play *Nathan the Wise*, 1779)

> Despise my people if you will.
> Neither I nor you have chosen our people. Are we
> Our people? People? What means then the people?
> Are Jew and Christian rather Jew and Christian.
> Than men?

B. (Napoleon, announcing his blockade 1806)

> England will find her vessels laden with useless wealth wandering round the high seas, where they claim to rule as sole masters, seeking in vain from the Sound to the Hellespont for a port to open and receive them.

EXERCISE 3

What point could be made to suggest that the successes of Felix Mendelssohn were not really a triumph for the emancipation of the Jews?

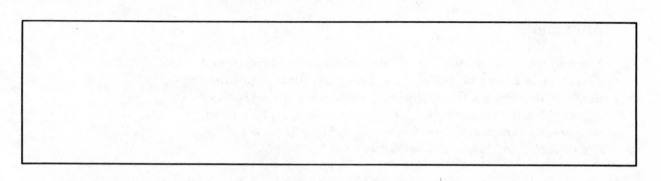

Fig. 21   Moses Mendelssohn.

SPECIMEN ANSWER

He was in fact baptized *as a Christian*. He might well not have been so successful had he remained a practising Jew. Note also that his father thought it better that he should change his name.

DISCUSSION

I simply put this question in to demonstrate the dangers and difficulties in history of talking in a facile way about such broad trends as 'the emancipation of the Jews'. Persecution of, and hostility to, the Jews, as we know, long continued. On the other hand, *something* has happened between Moses, child of the ghetto, and Felix, idol of Berlin, and, soon, of London too.

(Suggested break)

Fig. 22 Mendelssohn playing before Queen Victoria and the Prince Consort at Buckingham Palace.

SECTION 3

MUSICOLOGY AND ITS ORIGIN IN THE EARLY NINETEENTH CENTURY

INTRODUCTION

If you hear a composer who is a good solo performer playing from his own manuscript, or from a printed score of it, you may reasonably assume that the performance you experience is 'authoritative'. By 'authoritative' I mean that both *text* (the notes he plays) and *interpretation* (how he plays them) have authority. No one else is likely to produce a more authoritative performance. Other musicians, of course, may produce first-class performances, but the musical *author*, if he is a good performer, has an *authority* which others can hardly be expected to challenge.

The same is true if the composer is conducting or directing others in a performance of his music. If he is recording the music for a gramophone company he will be especially careful to ensure that nothing is 'frozen' into perpetuity that does not meet with his approval. He knows that such a recording will be considered 'authoritative' in both text and interpretation, and that it is his responsibility to detect flaws in the performance. Admittedly, he may not have a completely free hand in remedying defects. The performers and the recording studio will have been booked for a fixed period of time at a fixed cost. The composer cannot disregard such practical considerations in performance any more than in composition itself. There are always constraints of some sort on the creative artist.

EXERCISE 1

You have just read the arts page of a national newspaper. Two concerts are reviewed and by a coincidence each contained a piece of music which was reviewed also in your local weekly paper *The Little Worthington Informer*. This piece of music reviewed by all three was the *Piano Sonata 1970* by John Henry Adams. Had you been able to attend one of these concerts, at which do you think you would have heard the most 'authoritative' performance? Put A in the appropriate box. Put B for the runner-up and C for the performance you think would have been least 'authoritative'. Of course, if you think two of them were equally authoritative, use the same letter twice. Here are the reviews:

1   'Mr Jones is a well-known advocate of contemporary music. It would be hard to imagine a more sympathetic performance of the *Piano Sonata 1970* by John Henry Adams than the one Mr Jones gave at the Royal Festival Hall last night. This fine one-movement Sonata, the last item in a long and difficult programme performed entirely from memory, was played faultlessly (I was following the score) and with splendid insight into this composer's style. Mr Adams, who arrived just in time to hear his work, acknowledged the applause of the large audience and seemed delighted with the performance.'

2   'Little Worthington does not often have the chance to hear modern music and perhaps this is just as well. We would rather have silence than the cacophony we heard last night masquerading as the *Piano Sonata 1970* by John Henry Adams. Mrs Worthington's daughter, Alicia, (who is at present in her first year at the Greater Worthington Piano Academy, having been dissuaded from pursuing a stage career) spent a full fifteen minutes of her otherwise delightful recital on Mr Adams' discordant and meaningless music. If only she had spent the time to advantage by giving us some more pieces like Mrs Worthington's own *Elfin Dance* and *Fiddler's Fancy*, both of which were rapturously received by the large audience of about sixty members of the Preservation Society, we would not have had a single word of criticism. The flower decorations were by Mrs Jackson and contributed much to the sense of occasion.'

3   'Last night, at the *London Society for the Promotion of New Piano Music*, we heard John Henry Adams perform from memory his *Piano Sonata 1970*. This piece came first in a long programme in which various composers played their own music. Mr Adams has an enviable reputation as a composer and this Sonata will no doubt add to it when we get to know the piece better. Mr Adams is scarcely his own best advocate, however, and the performance sounded slipshod and hurried – almost as if the composer were striving to keep an appointment elsewhere.'

ANSWER

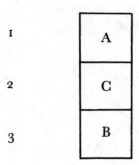

DISCUSSION

If you thought the first reported performance would have been the most authoritative one I would agree with you. Mr. Jones has a reputation for playing contemporary music (the inference being that he plays it well) and on this particular occasion he seems to have excelled himself. Both text and interpretation appear to have been observed impeccably. The composer's presence does not affect the authority of a performance, by the way. Composers must sometimes happen to attend poor performances of their music, but they can hardly show their displeasure publicly.

It is more than likely that the next most authoritative performance would have been the composer's. Of course, if only Mr. Adams were a first-class pianist, his performance would have had an authority which even Mr. Jones could hardly be expected to achieve. But clearly Mr. Adams is not a very good pianist; it seems he has played his music badly on previous occasions. Although interpretation may be as important, or perhaps more so, than textual accuracy (no one minds the occasional wrong note) we can hardly accept a 'hurried and slipshod' performance as being potentially authoritative.

Miss Worthington's performance was probably the least authoritative, for it is unrealistic to expect a young girl in her first year of full-time musical study to perform a difficult modern work with the kind of authority Mr. Jones possesses, and even though Mr. Adams didn't play the piano very well, he was, after all, the composer and we cannot deny his performance a fair degree of authority.

The fact that both Mr. Jones and the composer played from memory is immaterial. Don't let this confuse your understanding of what I said in the very first paragraph. Many professional musicians are able to hold every detail of a work in their heads; in fact, they may well play better for doing so, since they are freed from the visual concept of the music and can concentrate entirely on the aural and formal aspects. When I wrote 'If you hear a composer . . . playing from his own manuscript . . .' I meant that he may either do just this, or else that his performance will be based on it if he plays from memory.

You may argue that the above exercise has a fundamental weakness: that the evidence depended upon the critics' views, so how do we know what really took place? Well, of course, we don't know for certain that any criticisms we read are a true account of what actually happened artistically, because all criticism contains an element of subjectivity. Nevertheless, I think we may reasonably take it that critics writing in the national papers are responsible. Our first critic would hardly say that 'Mr. Jones is a well-known advocate of contemporary music' if this were demonstrably false, and similarly the other critic writing of Mr. Adams' performance seems to have had cause to comment on this composer's apparently long-standing inability to perform his own music well. The case of the critic writing in *The Little Worthington Informer* is different. The writer is biased against modern music, favours home-made trivia, and mixes descriptions of flower-arrangements with musical criticism. I took no notice of this in my discussion of Miss Worthington's performance, relying for my decision entirely upon the facts which were likely to be substantially correct: that Miss Worthington was young, in her first year of studying towards what was for her a second-choice career, and that her performance, however good, was unlikely to match either of the others in its authority.

The conclusion we can draw from the above exercise is that no one, not even a composer, can give an authoritative performance if he is not a good performer. Now read the first paragraph of this section of the unit again, please.

EXERCISE 2

Here are three imaginary record reviews. They each refer to the same modern symphony, and are concerned with its performance, not with its artistic value. This is a point I have to make, for some reviewers concentrate on discussing the nature of a particular composition, whereas others concentrate on a performance of it. There is room for both types of musical criticism, but for the purposes of this exercise, we are concerned with the second. Which recording do you think is likely to be the most authoritative one? Write A, B or C in the boxes provided, as you did in the previous exercise, but this time justify your grading by some short comments in the larger boxes. Then compare your grades and comments with mine.

1   'The orchestra responds magnificently under the composer's direction, demonstrating yet again that this musician is as at home on the rostrum as he is pursuing his craft as a composer. A fine recording in every respect.'

2   'A fine performance of the Symphony. Herr Rudolfstein takes the slow movement much slower than in the composer's recent recording (which follows the metronomic indication)[1] but the rich tone of the strings and the excellent chording of woodwind and brass give the movement a warmth which fully justify such treatment.'

3   'A virtuosic performance by the Ars Nova Symphony Orchestra under their conductor Philip Vitry. The breakneck speed at which this conductor takes the final movement shows this orchestra off to particular advantage. Every note is audible and the effect is electrifying. The performing time is twelve minutes less than the composer's own recording, which in itself gives an indication of this orchestra's astonishing technical skill.'

1   A metronome is a device which can indicate exactly how many beats occur each minute. The composer can thus give precise indications of the speeds he wants. For example, ♩ =60 means there should be 60 crotchets each minute, or one each second.

1 This composer is clearly a first-rate conductor. The orchestra responds to him in this capacity 'magnificently' and the critic tells us that 'yet again' the composer has shown himself to be equally at home as a conductor. We may assume this is an 'authoritative' performance.

A

2 What right has Mr. Rudolfstein to ignore the composer's own metronomic indications? Why should this conductor know better? Nevertheless, the orchestra seems to play well and perhaps the lack of comment on the other movements implies that Rudolfstein's performance follows the score more faithfully in these than in the second movement. Rather a difficult one this, but I'd give it B rather than C.

B

3 Everything I'm told about this performance makes me feel that the composer comes last in the list of priorities, musical and otherwise. The conductor and orchestra seem to want to show themselves off to advantage rather than the music, and I cannot think a performance that takes 12 minutes less than the composer's (remember this is a 3-movement symphony not a 3-act opera) is very 'authoritative'.

C

DISCUSSION

It was fairly obvious that 1 was the most authoritative recording. You should have given this A, and if by any chance you didn't then re-read the first two paragraphs of this section. Recordings 2 and 3 are harder to choose between and if you gave either of them B or C I would not quibble with you. Perhaps I was put off by the racy wording of the third reviewer and took too much for granted in what the second wrote. Nevertheless, I stick to my opinions and you are entitled to yours. The important point is that no one could rightly argue that the first recording was not the most authoritative.

MUSICOLOGY

I have talked about text and interpretation. Let us consider the matter of text more closely. The contemporary composer may play or conduct his music from his own manuscript. More probably, he will use a printed score. However, this printed score will have been made from his autograph manuscript and checked by him. To all intents and purposes, therefore, the autograph and the printed score of a modern musical work are synonymous. Both may be regarded as *primary source material*. Nevertheless, the researcher would need to examine both texts, manuscript and printed, because composers and printers are fallible. There may be mistakes in the printed score that the composer has not noticed. Likewise, the autograph may contain minor errors that the printer has corrected. The great opera composer Verdi (1813–1901) conducted from printed scores made from his manuscripts without, it seems, ever noticing the large number of differences between the two which modern research has identified.

Broadly speaking, music by living composers presents few textual or interpretative problems. Music by composers of recent memory likewise presents few *textual* problems, but if they lived before it was possible to record music, or even if they recorded some works and not others, then *interpretative* problems may already have arisen. I believe that very few people – perhaps one or two exceptional conductors or other professional musicians – can recall exactly how Elgar (1857–1934) conducted *The Dream of Gerontius*, or how Ravel (1875–1937) played much of his piano music. This is despite the fact that Elgar recorded some of his own music (for example, the *Enigma Variations*) and Ravel some of his piano music. If problems of text and interpretation arise when performing music by men who died as recently as Elgar and Ravel, then you will appreciate how much greater the problems are when we perform music by men like Bach and Handel, long since dead.

With the exception of a few perceptive professionals, most people living before the nineteenth century did not regard what little earlier music they knew as being of much consequence. In 1776 Charles Burney, organist, composer and distinguished man of letters, published the first volume of his epoch-making four-volume *A General History of Music*. He possessed a vast first-hand knowledge of European music, old and new, but true to the spirit of his age, he rated contemporary music most highly. He had this to say of Elizabethan instrumental music (which today we regard as including some of the finest composed at that time by any nation):

'The instrumental music of Queen Elizabeth's reign seems to partake of the pedantry and foppery of the times; eternal fugues upon dry and unmeaning subjects were the means of establishing reputation for learning and contrivance.'

At the time he wrote his history, Burney did not think very highly of Bach either:

'[Bach] never stooped to the easy and graceful. I have never seen a fugue by this learned and powerful author upon a motive that is natural and *chantant* [singing], or even an easy and obvious passage that is not loaded with crude and difficult accompaniments.'

But when he comes to writing about his contemporary Joseph Haydn (1732–1809) he becomes ecstatic:

'The admirable, the matchless Haydn! for whose productions I have received more pleasure late in life when tired of most other music, than I ever received in the most ignorant and rapturous part of my youth when everything was new and the disposition to be pleased undiminished by criticism or satiety.'

Haydn, of course, deserves such praise – but not at the expense of his predecessors.

In the eighteenth century, and previously, composers were regarded as master-craftsmen, hired to provide new music for a sacred or secular establishment. This meant writing the music, rehearsing and performing it, and keeping the musical instruments in good condition. Haydn served the noble, rich, Hungarian Esterházy family in this way from 1761 until his death nearly half-a-century later, under favourable conditions; Bach served the council at St. Thomas's Church, Leipzig (which at the time of his appointment noted that as the best musicians were not available it would have to make do with an average one) from 1723 until his death in 1750, under generally unfavourable conditions. Both men, like countless other *Kapellmeisters* and *Cantors*, provided their employers with a constant stream of new music. There must have been specific exceptions, but in general, music by their predecessors, by other contemporaries, or even their own last-year's music, would have been less acceptable. It would have seemed second-hand, and they were being paid to provide new material. The reason for this is that art was not then regarded as something apart from everyday existence. It was as natural to discard the old art as it is for today's society (or at least, the advertisers' image of it) to discard last year's clothes, motor-car and washing-machine. The one musical area in which this still happens is that of pop music – which, while perhaps admitting some degree of commercial persuasion, nevertheless tells us something about its relevance to today's teenagers.

So when Bach died, much of his music died with him – although you might not think this judging from the enormous amount which survives. It survives largely by accident however. Some of the plates of music which Bach had engraved himself were melted down by one of his sons for ready cash; some of his manuscripts were reputedly used as wrappings for groceries; even his considerable correspondence with the great French composer François Couperin (1668–1733), none of which survives, was later used, it is said, by the Couperin family to cover pots of home-made jam. You don't need to have any great love for Bach's music to feel horrified by such disrespect for precious historical documents. Furthermore, Bach's case is typical rather than exceptional. But the crucial point is that these documents were not considered important by Bach's immediate successors. Although Bach had a great reputation as a performer (which was no doubt talked of long after his death), as a composer, he was considered old-fashioned and rather dull, even while alive. Why should his sons, pupils or others of the next generation have preserved his music any more than his hat, coat and shoes?

(Suggested break)

So it was, that after one performance on Good Friday 1729, Bach's huge *St. Matthew Passion* was neglected. Very little of Bach's music was published, and since no publisher would have undertaken the *St. Matthew Passion* for obvious commercial reasons, the work remained in manuscript. It survived the hazards of time along with its companion the *St. John Passion*, but the *St. Luke Passion* and *St. Mark Passion* were lost. Enthusiasm for some of Bach's music was nevertheless kept alive by a handful of 'initiates' and passed on from generation to generation. Felix Mendelssohn's own teacher, Karl Zelter, had studied with Johann Kirnberger, who in turn had been a pupil of Johann Sebastian Bach himself. We may be sure that Zelter's own enthusiasm for Bach's music arose in this way.

Felix Mendelssohn, then, as a pupil of Zelter, got to know Bach's music while still a boy. Several references he made to it in early letters show that he fully appreciated its importance and that he even based his opinion of others on their knowledge, or lack of knowledge, of it. Thus in a letter to Zelter dated September 13, 1822, when Felix was 13, he wrote '. . . it was delightful to make the acquaintance of Professor Kaiser . . . He has a good piano, the Handel Suites and many of his fugues, and the *Well-Tempered Clavier* of Bach, and he loves both enthusiastically.' (*The Well-Tempered Clavier* is a collection of forty-eight preludes and fugues for keyboard; often known simply as 'The Forty-Eight', it is one of Bach's greatest achievements.) Remembering that Bach's music was not generally known or appreciated at the time, you will realize that Mendelssohn's observation was both precocious and astute. In a letter to his sister Fanny, dated April 20, 1825, and written from Paris, he laments the current standards of musical taste there: 'You say, Fanny, that I should become a missionary and convert Onslow and Reiche [prominent composers] to a love for Beethoven and Sebastian Bach. That is just what I am endeavouring to do. But remember, my dear child, that these people do not know a single note of *Fidelio* [Beethoven's only opera] and believe Bach to be nothing but a wig stuffed with learning'.

As you will learn in the first television programme, the boy Mendelssohn used to go to Zelter's house on Friday evenings where a handful of enthusiasts would sing what Zelter called the 'bristly bits' of Bach. Here he came to know some of Zelter's treasures –

music which Zelter seems to have guarded closely, not in a miserly way, but because he felt it was up to him to preserve what the world at large no longer valued. Mendelssohn valued this music however. It included a score of Bach's *St. Matthew Passion*, a copy of which he longed to possess for himself. He was successful, for when he was only fourteen he persuaded his grandmother to have the work copied, and the new score was given to him as a Christmas present in 1824. It later became his burning desire to perform it and this, as we know, he eventually accomplished too. Eduard Devrient sang the part of Jesus in the performance. In his *Recollections*[1] he writes of Zelter's opposition to the project, and tells how Mendelssohn and he, Devrient, overcame it. Zelter's 'opposition', however, was merely that of a museum curator who feared to devalue a precious exhibit by making it generally available to an uncritical public. Once he had given the project his blessing, he gave Mendelssohn every help both administrative and musical, discreetly and generously withdrawing to give Mendelssohn full credit as the performance approached. This is worth mentioning, for history seems to have dealt harshly with Zelter; furthermore, he is often referred to as an antiquarian and teacher, which although true, is only half true. Zelter was also a practising musician and composer, whose songs Goethe considered superior to those of Franz Schubert.

Let Mendelssohn's sister, Fanny, take up the story at this point; she is writing to Carl Klingemann, a close friend of the family, and the letter[2] is dated March 22, 1829, the day after the repeat performance of Bach's *St. Matthew Passion*:

'Felix and Devrient had been talking for a long time of the possibility of a representation, but the plan had neither form nor shape until one evening at our house they settled the affair, and walked off the next morning in brand-new yellow kid gloves (very important in their eyes) to the managers of the academy. They very carefully minced the matter, and in all possible discreetness put the question whether they might be allowed the use of the concert-hall for a charitable purpose. In that case, and as the music they were going to perform was likely to be very successful, they offered to give a second performance for the benefit of the academy. This the gentlemen declined with thanks, and preferred to insist on a fixed payment of fifty thalers, leaving the profits to the disposal of the concert-givers. By-the-by, they are still ruminating over that reply of theirs! Zelter made no objections, and the rehearsals began on the Friday following. Felix went over the whole score, made a few judicious cuts, and only instrumented the recitative, 'And the veil of the temple was rent in twain.' Everything else was left untouched. The people were astonished, stared, admired; and when, after a few weeks, the rehearsals in the academy itself commenced, their faces became *very* long with surprise at the existence of such a work, about which they, the members of the Berlin Academy, knew nothing. After having got over their astonishment, they began to study with true, warm interest. The thing itself, the novelty and originality of the form, took hold of them, the subject was universally comprehensible and engaging, and Devrient sang the recitatives most beautifully. The genial spirit

1   Eduard Devrient, *My Recollections of Felix Mendelssohn-Bartholdy and his Letters to Me*, translated by Natalia MacFarren; Richard Bentley, London, 1869.

2   Sebastian Hensel, *The Mendelssohn Family (1729–1747)*, translated by Carl Klingemann, Sampson Low and Co., London, 1881, pp. 170–173.

and enthusiasm evinced by all the singers during the very first rehearsals, and which each new rehearsal kindled to ever-increasing love and ardour; the delight and surprise created by each new element – the solos, the orchestra, Felix's splendid interpretation and his accompanying the first rehearsals at the piano from beginning to end *by heart*, all these were moments never to be forgotten. Zelter, who had lent his help at the first rehearsals, gradually retreated, and during the later rehearsals, as well as at the concerts, with praiseworthy resignation took his seat among the audience. And now the members of the academy themselves spread such a favourable report about the music, and such a general and vivid interest was created in all classes, that on the very day after the first advertisement of the concert all the tickets were taken, and during the latter days upwards of a thousand people applied in vain. On Wednesday, March 10,[1] the first representation took place, and excepting a few slight mistakes of the solo-singers it may be called a perfect success. We were the first in the orchestra. As soon as the doors were opened, the people, who already had been long waiting outside, rushed into the hall, which was quite full in less than a quarter of an hour. I sat at the corner, where I could see Felix very well, and had gathered the strongest alto-voices around me. The choruses were sung with a fire, a striking power, and also with a touching delicacy and softness the like of which I have never heard, except at the second concert, when they surpassed themselves. Taking for granted that you still remember its dramatic form, I send you a textbook, just mentioning that the account of the evangelist was sung by Stümer, the words of Jesus by Devrient, of Peter by Bader, the High-priest and Pilate by Busolt, Judas by Weppler. Mmes. Schätzel, Milder, and Türr-schmiedt sang the soprano and alto parts exquisitely. The room was crowded, and had all the air of a church: the deepest quiet and most solemn devotion pervaded the whole, only now and then involuntary utterances of intense emotion were heard. What is so often erroneously maintained of such like undertakings truly and fully applies to this one, that a peculiar spirit and general higher interest prevaded the concert, that everybody did his duty to the best of his powers, and many did more. Rietz, for instance, who with the help of his brother and brother-in-law had undertaken to copy the parts of all the different instruments, refused all pay for himself and the other two. Most singers declined accepting the tickets offered to them, or else paid for them; so that for the first concert only six free tickets were issued (of which Spontini had two), and for the second none at all. Even before the first concert the many who had not been able to gain admission raised a loud cry for a repetition, and the industrial schools petitioned to subscribe; but by this time Spontini was on the alert, and—with the greatest amiability—tried to prevent a second performance. Felix and Devrient, however, took the straightest course, and procured an order from the crown-prince, who from the beginning had taken a lively interest in the enterprise, and so the concert was repeated on Saturday, March 21, Bach's birthday: the same crowd, and a still greater audience, for the ante-room and the small rehearsal-room behind the audience were added, and all tickets sold. The choruses were perhaps still more exquisite than the first time, the instruments splendid; only one sad mistake of Milder's, and a few slight short-comings in the solos, put a damp on Felix's spirits – but on the whole I may say that better success could not be desired.'

---

1 It was really March 11.

Fanny Mendelssohn married Wilhelm Hensel in October of 1829, and it was their son, Sebastian Hensel, who wrote the book from which the above letter is taken. Fanny was an accomplished musician, by the way, some of whose songs were published in her brother's name (a woman would hardly have published them herself at this time) and we may accept that in musical matters at least, she knew what she was talking about. So while her letter shows a sisterly enthusiasm for Felix's success, the musical facts are likely to be correct and unadorned.

Of course, no event of consequence is without an antecedent, and in this case it was partly the biography of J. S. Bach by Johann Nickolaus Forkel which created an interest in Bach's music and helped to prepare the way for Mendelssohn. In 1777 Forkel had been appointed Professor of Musical History at Göttingen, and his biography was published in 1802 when only a handful of Bach's pieces were generally known. As the late Professor Redlich has stated:[1]

> 'Forkel's book did much to conjure up the forgotten figure of the great Thomas Cantor [J. S. Bach] who died in 1750 and of whose music less than ten publications were in circulation. The revival of interest in the music of J. S. Bach, starting up everywhere between roughly 1788 and 1813 and culminating in groups of enthusiasts crystallising in Britain and Germany, brings matters to a head, as far as musical research is concerned. The necessity of having to search for Bach's autographs, authenticated copies, rare first prints and variants, lead to a new kind of musical philology and critical scholarship. In 1829 Mendelssohn performed, for the first time after a full century, Bach's *St. Matthew Passion* in Berlin in Holy Week. The sensational success of that performance clinched the matter. Scattered reprints and first publications of some of Bach's works were followed by the foundation of the English and German Bach Societies in 1849 and 1850. In the latter year the German Bach Society started to publish the complete and critical edition of Bach's works, an undertaking which came to its end fifty years later, in 1900. With its last volume, musicology had become a discipline admitted to universities in Germany and France.'

The distinguished musicologist Friedrich Blume in his article *Bach in the Romantic Era*[2] also stresses the importance of Mendelssohn's achievement:

> 'Thus Mendelssohn becomes the pivotal figure in the Romantic appreciation of Bach, and his work marks the historical moment of final adoption. With that adoption, neither the older rationalistic conception nor the historical interest disappeared; but both were surmounted by an enthusiastic devotion that saw in Bach more than the embodiment of eternal laws, saw in him the subtle interpreter and promoter of 'rare states of the soul' (Schumann) and for this reason became faithful to the letter of his works. This truly romantic encounter with Bach left an indelible mark in the history of the Bach revival. The most divergent minds became united in their enthusiasm for Bach, which both furthered and beclouded the appreciation of his music for a long time to come.'

1   H. F. Redlich, *The Meaning and the Aims of Musicology* (Percival Lecture), from vol. 106 of 'Memoirs & Proceedings of the Manchester Literary and Philosophical Society', Session 1963–64.

2   *Musical Quarterly* 50, 1964.

This block is about Bach or Mendelssohn only in so far as the Bach-Mendelssohn performance of nearly 150 years ago crystallized a change of attitude that has had two important results for us today. The second of these – the fact that most of the concert music performed today is by dead composers – we shall mention in the final section. The first, however, is that all this early music has been made available to us by the rise of the discipline of musicology whose prime importance has been the recovery of textual and interpretative information about the music of the past, necessitated by the growing desire of musicians and audiences alike for performances of such music. At first the text was more or less all that mattered. Performances were often coloured by the 'Romantic' view of the past, which as with many aspects of Romanticism, was paradoxical. It was hard for early nineteenth-century enthusiasts to reconcile the seemingly unparalleled skill and imagination of a composer like Bach with their current belief in progress. To balance this problem of eighteenth-century genius and nineteenth-century progress, it was necessary to admit that earlier composers had been hampered by the circumstances in which they had lived and worked. This enabled up-to-date recreations of their music, enlarged and inflated possibly beyond recognition, to be made in the belief that had they been alive they would have taken advantage of improved instruments, larger orchestras, and 'progress' in general. This argument, by no means rare even today, is fallacious, since had Bach or Handel lived in a later age they would have composed different music.

We shall discuss Mendelssohn's performance of Bach's *St. Matthew Passion* more fully later; but in the light of general trends, his concern for, and adherence to, Bach's original conception is all the more remarkable. In fact, it was Handel's music with its immediate dramatic appeal, even more than Bach's, which encouraged inflated performances. In the case of Handel, who unlike Bach was enormously successful during his own lifetime (and achieved early recognition as England's national composer), his music was never entirely forgotten, merely transformed through 'bigger and better' performances, especially those given during the Handel Commemoration Festivals held in Westminster Abbey, starting in 1784. In our first radio programme we shall investigate the matter of 'inflated *versus* authentic' performances more fully, by tracing the performance history of one well-known work – Handel's celebrated oratorio *The Messiah*.

Let us now attempt a definition of musicology. Whereas we can regard musical composition and performance as the *practice* of music, musicology is the *science* of music, embracing all aspects of musical history, particularly those relating to the transcription and editing of manuscript and early printed copies. Closely allied with such studies (often called musical palaeography) are problems of interpretation and performance. These include matters like the exact nature of early instruments and how performance-practices varied in different times and places. Evidence may be found in a variety of ways: for example, by studying musical forms and methods of composition, by reading early treatises on music, by examining records of musical and other institutions, and, of course, by studying the original texts of the music itself. The emphasis is upon scientific investigation of a kind similar to that used by scholars in other fields and free from emotive judgements and mere speculation.

(Suggested break)

Fig. 23 *The Prince Consort playing the organ before Queen Victoria and Mendelssohn at Buckingham Palace, 1842.*

47

SECTION 4

SOURCE MATERIAL IN MUSIC

In the following section we shall consider how the musicologist-editor handles source material and some of the problems that face him when transcribing old music.

If we accept that one of the functions of musicology – perhaps its prime function – is to recover the great music of the past, then it follows that the musicologist must be able to present it to the modern reader, whether scholar or performer, in such a way that it is possible to see at once what the composer's original wishes were and what suggestions or corrections the editor has made. It is the editor's responsibility to provide full documentary evidence.

One of the main problems facing the editor of old music is that musical notation itself has changed, and early music may be intelligible only to a specialist. (As we have noted previously, this was probably one of the stumbling blocks facing the Romantics who wanted to get to know more about mediaeval and renaissance music). Such a specialist, or musical paleographer, must be able to transcribe music written in a number of different systems. It is true that the corner-stones of staff notation were laid in around 1050 and that it had more or less reached its present-day form in the early seventeenth century. The problem, however, is that between those dates many types of staff notation (and even other notations) arose and withered. When we come to edit the music of Bach or Handel, we have few problems as far as the notes themselves are concerned.

Of course, reading anyone else's handwriting can be troublesome; but as you can see from this extract from Bach's own autograph of the *St. Matthew Passion*, even Bach's music manuscript is something of a work of art:

Fig. 24

49

Handel's manuscripts, on the other hand, are seldom as attractive as Bach's. Here are the closing bars of *Messiah*:

Fig. 25

Thus apart from possible handwriting difficulties, there are relatively few problems of actual transcription in music written since about 1600. There may, of course, be crucial problems relating to its performance. The biggest of these is the problem of the early musical score not telling the whole story as it usually does today. Works that appear to have been composed for voices alone were often accompanied by instruments. This was common performance-practice, so the composer did not bother to mention it. Oboes and bassoons are often absent in eighteenth-century scores because these instruments frequently doubled violins and cellos where practicable. Again, musicians knew this, so composers did not spell it out. There may be problems too of lack of performance instructions relating to speed, dynamics and phrasing.

The chief problems of musical transcription occur in the period of about 1250–1600. In these 350 years we find a variety of musical notations. A composer living in 1600 might be unable to read music written by his own countrymen a century earlier. An English composer of the fourteenth century would have been unable to read Italian music of his own day, because the Italians had their own system of staff notation, so complicated that it died a natural death. Furthermore, staff notation of one kind or another was not the only system used. Here is a facsimile of the original manuscript of the *In Dulci Jubilo* setting which we discussed in *Form and Meaning*:

Fig. 26

The above is a mixture of staff notation and letter notation, and is called *Old German Organ Tablature*. A tablature is a system of notation which uses letters, figures, numbers, or other symbols to represent the music. Occasionally, as in the above example, it is used in conjunction with staff notation. There were various kinds of tablature to suit various musical instruments.

One of the most popular types of music in the sixteenth century was lute music. Over 2000 pieces survive from England alone. Lute music had its own Lute Tablature, and even this broke down further into French, Italian, Spanish and German types, all different and requiring specialist attention. Here is an extract from the beautiful *Melancholy Galliard* by John Dowland (1563–1626), who like all English lute composers wrote in French Lute Tablature.

51

Fig. 27

(Incidentally, each set of six horizontal lines in the above example represents the six double-strings or 'courses' of the lute. The similarity to staff notation is a coincidence. The letter *a* denotes an open string, *b* the semitone higher, *c* the whole tone higher, and so on.)

In the modern staff notation, the opening bars of that music would look like this:

Fig. 28

Tablatures still survive today in popular sheet music. You may have seen those 'chord boxes' which show a guitarist *how* to produce a given chord. These now usually appear in conjunction with staff-notation so that when you buy an arrangement of a pop song, you can accompany it either on the piano or else on the guitar.

You might think that tablatures were superior to staff notation because they tell you *how* to produce music and not just *what* music should be produced. This is true, but they have one overriding disadvantage: unlike staff notation, the visual effect of a tablature bears little relation to the musical structure it represents. Musical analysis, or even mere identification, is difficult if tablatures are used.

As I have already mentioned, staff notation itself has undergone many changes. Here is a facsimile of a manuscript containing the beautiful three-voice song *O Rosa Bella* (*O Beautiful Rose*) by the outstanding English composer John Dunstable (died 1453) who enjoyed a great reputation throughout Europe:

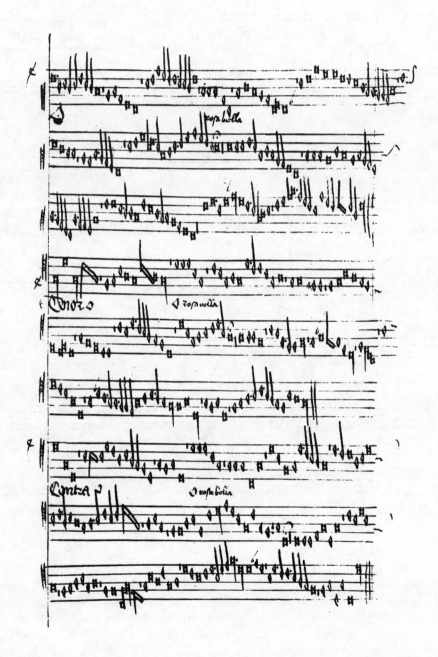

Fig. 29

The three-voice parts, the top part, the alto or contratenor part, and the tenor part are all written out separately as was customary at this time. The note-shapes include *ligatures*, that is, two or more notes joined together, and the values of the notes are determined by the way these ligatures are drawn. I have transcribed the opening of this piece so that you may see how it looks in modern notation:

Notes: "Discantus", "Contratenor" and "Tenor" are the usual names used for each "Voice" in three-part medieval music. It is unlikely that the contratenor and tenor parts are intended to be sung in this arrangement, since these parts are much more instrumental in character; the opening words are probably given merely as a cue for the players. G.H.

Fig. 30

The source material itself – manuscripts and printed books – is mostly in libraries. Some is in private collections. The editor's first task when producing a modern edition is to identify all the surviving sources. The most usual starting point is a previous edition (the information about sources is likely to be inadequate, however, for if it were otherwise there might be no need for a new edition) or else a scholarly book on the composer, a learned article, or an entry in one of the big multi-volume dictionaries like the English *Grove's Dictionary of Music and Musicians* or the German *Die Musik in Geschichte und Gegenwart*. The editor will need to follow up all such references to source material for himself. This may take him to the great collections in the British Museum, London; the Bodleian Library, Oxford; the Fitzwilliam Museum, Cambridge; and so on. There are also renowned music collections abroad of course, such as those in the library of the Paris Conservatoire, and in the New York Public Library, to give just two examples. In addition, the editor may have to visit minor collections in public or private hands. One thing is certain: he will need to search and examine much material in addition to that already identified by other scholars in the hope of discovering hitherto unknown material. His edition, therefore, may reflect only a very small part of his researches.

In general there are two types of edition of early music. First there is the edition, all too familiar to music students, which makes no distinction between the composer's own text and the editor's additions to it. The unsuspecting performer follows both with equal care believing that by playing this passage *piano*, that passage *forte*, another passage *legato*, and the final chord *arpeggio*, he is observing the wishes of the composer, when, as Professor Thurston Dart has written,[1] such instructions may be 'merely those of Herr X or Dr. Y, or even of Herr X, amended by Dr. Y, and thoroughly revised by the eminent pianist Mr. Z'.

So many of these editions sprang up during the last quarter of the nineteenth century, that I suspect they arose as a result of a renowned performer wishing to place his performance with all its idiosyncrasies, before as wide a public as possible. Today he would do this by making a gramophone record. Furthermore, in the nineteenth century performers took greater liberties with contemporary scores than they do today, and any such edition therefore would reflect these considerable divergencies from the autograph or first edition. Let us look at one small example of what I have been saying. Here is the autograph of the beginning of the renowned Polonaise in A Major written in 1838–9 by Frederick Chopin (1810–1849):

---

[1] Thurston Dart, *The Interpretation of Music*, Hutchinson's University Library, London, 1954, p. 18.

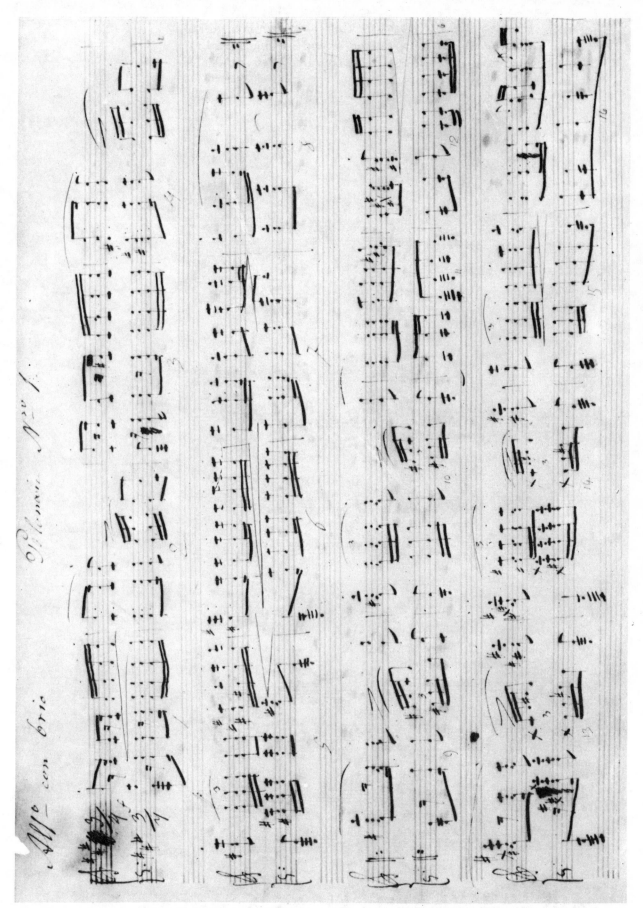

Fig. 31

Next, two editions of that music, the first (a) by the Hungarian pianist Rafael Joseffy (1853–1915), the second (b) by Hermann Scholtz (whose dates I cannot trace, but which I believe are broadly the same):

Fig. 32

Fig. 33

Even a brief glance at the autograph and then at either of the editions will reveal discrepancies between them. For example:

JOSEFFY'S EDITION

I		subtitle *Militaire* added
2	bar I	staccato dot (·) omitted over first right-hand chord (a staccato dot implies that the duration of a note or chord should be less than its notated value)
3	bars I, 3, 4, 6	left-hand staccato dots added (in accordance with Chopin's intentions no doubt, but not distinguishable in the text from the composer's directions)
4	bar 3	staccato dot omitted over first right-hand chord
5	bar 3	crescendo hairpin (<) added
6	bar 3	last chord in the right hand has wrong bottom note, similarly, top note of left-hand chord
7	bar 6	slur (⌒) omitted in right hand between first two chords (a slur means 'play this smoothly')
8	bar 7 (beat I)	slur added between first two chords possibly contradicting Chopin's intentions
9	bar 7	unnecessary accidentals (♮) added
10	bar 7 (beat 3)	more slurs added
11	bar 8	staccato dot omitted over first right-hand chord
12	bar 8	more unauthorized slurs
13		pedal marking added throughout (*Ped* means right, or 'sustaining' pedal down; * means release it)

SCHOLTZ'S EDITION

I	bar I	staccato dot omitted over first right-hand chord
2	bars I, 3, 4, 6	left-hand staccato dots added
3	bar 2	small accent or hairpin added between staves
4	bar 3	staccato dot omitted over first right-hand chord
5	bar 3 beat 3	crescendo hairpin added
6	bar 3	last chord in right hand has wrong bottom note, similarly top note of left-hand chord
7	bar 5	first chord has *ffz* added between staves (meaning 'very loud indeed with extra emphasis')
8	bar 6	small hairpin or accent added between staves

9	bar 7	*staccatissimo* mark (˙) meaning 'very short indeed' added over first chord in both hands
10	bar 7	hairpin added
11	bar 7	slurs added

(Both editions have added fingerings. This is helpful, provided a clear distinction is made between these and any original fingerings. This may seem a small matter, but in fact a composer's fingerings may give a considerable insight into the way in which he played the instrument and piece in question.)

You can see that there are about a dozen divergencies between eight bars of the autograph and eight bars of either edition. If we have identified so much unauthorized revision in so little music, what about the rest of the piece? Or the remainder of the music in the volume? Or the other volumes of Chopin's music that men like Joseffy and Scholtz may have edited? Or other collections of other composer's music they may have edited also? You can see that once the principle of unauthorized tampering with an author's text is allowed, it is not possible to feel confidence in any text that such an editor presents us with.

(Suggested break)

Fortunately, there is a type of edition which aims to be scrupulously faithful to the composer's intentions. It is known as an *Urtext* or *original text* edition. The text appears clean and uncluttered, and any additions, corrections or amendments that the editor has made in the light of his researches based on the autographs, surviving copies, and early editions, are clearly distinguishable from the composer's own text. The editor does this generally in one of three ways. He puts some information in square brackets, some information in small type and other information in italics. How he does this depends upon the musical context. For example, if he is supplying the composer's name or the title of the piece or perhaps a speed indication, all of which may be missing in an original source, he will normally put them in square brackets. If however he is adding an accidental he may put this in square brackets; but as this is a little clumsy, he will normally write a smaller accidental, one which is readily distinguishable from the full-size or original one. Similarly, with missing notes: these he will have engraved in small type so that they are readily distinguishable from the composer's own. If he adds expression marks like *piano* or *forte* – something he should only do very sparingly and then only to bring them in line with existing dynamic indications in other instruments in an orchestral score – he will normally italicize the word *piano* or *forte*, or else just the initial letter *p* or *f*.

Here is an example taken from such an edition. It is the last four bars of the second movement of Mozart's Sonata in D for two piano's, written in Vienna in 1781. The edition is by Ernst Fritz Schmid and published in 1955 by Bärenreiter of Leipzig as part of the New Edition of Mozart's music:

Fig. 34

NOTICE

1 accidental in brackets, therefore editorial

2 dynamics in bold type, therefore original

3 dynamic in italics, therefore editorial

4 phrasing dotted, therefore editorial

5 rest in brackets, therefore editorial

6 full-size *staccatissimo* mark (meaning 'play this note shorter than written') contrasts with

7 small-size *staccatissimo* mark, therefore editorial

All the editorial suggestions are valid, and both performers and scholars would welcome them. However, the editor has made it quite clear that these are his own suggestions and do not bear the composer's authority. That distinction is all-important, and enables us to place complete confidence in the rest of the text that he presents us with in Mozart's name.

You remember from our *Introduction to Music* that we mentioned how performance indications were not generally used by composers until the seventeenth and eighteenth centuries and that Italians were among the first to do so. Music by Bach, Handel and their numerous contemporaries has very few performance instructions – just the occasional speed, dynamic, and phrasing indications. These composers never used 'hairpin' markings. The further back in time you travel, the fewer performance indications you meet. The *Fitzwilliam Virginal Book*, of 1609–17 (from which the variations *Up Tails All* were taken) for example, has none at all. So if you meet an edition of old music which has a liberal sprinkling of performing instructions you may be fairly sure that these are editorial. The modern editor of 'collected editions' and the scholarly editor of smaller volumes, no longer adds performance indications liberally. He keeps them to a minimum. The cleaner and more uncluttered the text you see before you, therefore, the more likely it is to be the work of a good editor.

In a good 'critical' edition all major stages of editorial method should be clearly revealed. The editor should give reasons for decisions he may have taken. He will have written an introduction to the volume containing general and specific information about the origin of the music, the music itself, the sources, early and later printed editions, and so on, together with a section on editorial method perhaps with notes on the instruments, and some facsimiles of selected original texts. All significant divergencies between surviving sources will be collated in a Textual Commentary, usually found at the back of the volume, or else sometimes published as a companion volume so that it is possible to study music and written text simultaneously.

Let us look at a few bars of the same piece of music taken from a nineteenth-century edition and present-day one:

Fig. 35

The title page of that French edition, translated into English, reads like this: 'Collection Litolff/Keyboard Masters/Old Keyboard Music/Selected Works/Revised, fingered and phrased by Louis Köhler/Volume II/English, Italian and French schools/Braunschweig [place name]/Henry Litolff's Edition'. You will observe that there is no information about where the music in the volume has been found (it could even have been pirated from another edition) nor can we tell how much of the text and performing instructions are the composer's and how much the editor's. 'Revised, fingered and phrased' simply isn't good enough. What has been revised? Are any fingerings or phrasings original? We cannot tell. Here is that same piece of music again:

Prelude

Fig. 36

This time it is taken from the recent Collected Keyboard Music[1] of the composer.

EXERCISE

List at least three general ways in which the Litolff edition gives instructions to the performer which do not appear in the Collected Edition.

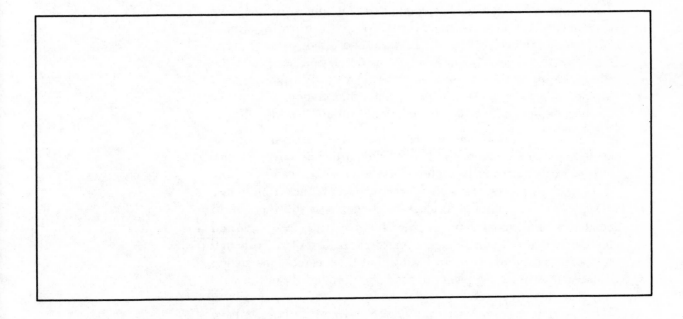

1 *Orlando Gibbons: Keyboard Music*, transcribed and edited by Gerald Hendrie, *Musica Britannica* XX (Stainer and Bell, London, 1962; second edition 1967).

SPECIMEN ANSWER

1 There is a speed direction *Allegro vivace*.

2 There are hairpin dynamic markings.

3 There is fingering.

4 There are several additional accidentals: two are 'cautionary' and do not matter much (the left-hand naturals in bars 3 and 6) but two change the character of the music (the left-hand sharps in bars 5 and 6).

DISCUSSION

You should have spotted the first three differences. Furthermore, you should by now appreciate that the first two *must* be the editor's suggestions and not the composer's, for as we have noted earlier, Italian terms did not make their way into music until the seventeenth and eighteenth centuries; and that hairpin dynamics were not used by Bach and Handel (both born in 1685) or their contemporaries, yet alone by composers writing a hundred years earlier. The fingering is editorial too, although in fact, some fingering is found in early music – all the more reason for the editor to show what he had added therefore. The blanket wording of the preface 'revised, fingered and phrased' is no substitute for editorial good manners: it is essential for any editor to be scrupulously fair to the author, especially if he is dead and cannot fight back, and to show precisely what is original and what is editorial.

Incidentally, if you glance at the second edition again you will see an editorial sharp, printed small, in bar 6, right hand. The editor is saying to the performer: 'I think it should be a sharp although there wasn't one in the text I took as my prime source for this piece. But if you look up the Textual Commentary at the end of the volume, I have listed precisely which sources had the sharp and which didn't. Take your own decision if you don't accept mine'. At the very beginning of the piece, between the staves, you can see the symbol ₵. This was the original time-signature, and although some time-signatures found in early music are not used today (which is why the editor has modernized them all – this is explained in the Editorial Method) they nevertheless provide useful information. The stroke through the symbol meant 'play this fast' – in other words, *Allegro*.

The task of establishing scholarly texts which are also of im-mediate use to a performer and which do not therefore require him to read explanations or footnotes unless he so wishes, can be a slow and laborious process. It is often necessary to produce a hierarchy of copyists and to establish which were professionals and which were amateurs. Professional copyists generally give better readings, and professional musicians, especially composers, the best of all; although composers sometimes write so hastily that their copies look messy. Amateurs, often having plenty of time, may produce beautiful texts which are nevertheless full of mistakes.

In the unique case of Orlando Gibbons, whose *Prelude* we have just discussed, there is not a single note of music surviving in his autograph, although some forty manuscript copies survive contain-ing keyboard music by him. In order to edit his music, it was necessary to find out whether any of the copyists had known the composer and made their manuscripts directly from his. Other questions had to be asked. For example, how authentic were the copyists' attributions? If it were not possible to rely on scribal evidence in a given instance, would stylistic analysis show if a piece ascribed to Gibbons were really by him? Would such an analysis reveal if such a piece were by him even if it was ascribed to someone else? To find answers it was necessary to examine every manuscript which might contain keyboard music of this period and many others besides; to transcribe a thousand texts to produce the fifty in the edition; to make a detailed stylistic analysis of all the keyboard music of Orlando Gibbons and his near contemporaries; and so on. Details of sources, and every significant variant between different sources of the same piece of music were collated and recorded in the Textual Commentary at the end of the book, so that scholars and performers alike could check for themselves the work that had been done and the decisions that had been taken.

If Orlando Gibbons presents the editor of his music with special problems because of the absence of any autograph texts, then George Frideric Handel[1] (1685–1759) poses special problems because of the embarrassing number of autograph and authorized texts which survive – sometimes several different ones for the same piece of music. Handel was not only a great composer: he was also a highly successful one. He employed a number of copyists to make further texts from his own manuscripts for performance, or presentation, or sale. He checked many of these further copies that his secretaries produced and directed performances from them. Thus these *secondary* sources have as much or more authority than the hastily written 'originals' and may be considered as *co-primary* with the originals.

To complicate matters further, there may be several 'originals' since Handel sometimes revised his music to accommodate different performance situations. His most famous work, *Messiah*, exists in several 'original' versions and poses a labyrinth of textual problems for the present-day editor.

Another such instance is the so-called Chandos Anthems[2] which Handel wrote between 1717 and 1719 for the first Duke of Chandos. The sixty sources so far identified include a complete set of autographs – as many as four differing autograph manuscripts for a single anthem – and between thirty and forty *co-primary* ones. All of these have to be dated, the authority of the autographs established beyond reasonable doubt, the various copyists identified wherever possible, and the whole mass of material collated in a handbook which accompanies the edition.

Not all editorial problems in music are as complicated as those of Orlando Gibbons and George Frideric Handel, who each represents an extreme case; I have chosen them because I have an intimate knowledge of the problems. Nevertheless, it is seldom a simple matter to produce an 'authoritative' text of the music of a composer who died more than 100 years ago. You might ask why we bother to do it at all, since it is clear that a composer like Handel did not mind revising his music to suit the occasion. Does it really matter whether or not we have an 'authoritative' or 'definitive' text of such music?

1   I follow Handel's own 'English' spelling of his name.

2   George Frideric Handel, the Chandos Anthems; edition being prepared by Gerald Hendrie for the *Hallische Händel Ausgabe* (Halle Handel Society) published by Bärenreiter of Leipzig. This is a 'Collected Edition'.

We shall investigate the phenomenon of varying but equally valid performances of the same piece of music later in this study. Closely allied to this question, however, is the fact that whereas many twentieth-century composers expect performers to follow the musical score and interpretations precisely, composers of earlier periods expected the performer to contribute his own ideas. Performers would ornament their parts, additional instruments might be added, or others substituted. A keyboard player, who in Handel's day directed the performance and played continuously to keep things together, was known as the *continuo* player. He would 'realize' the shorthand which was often all the composer gave him and interpret it according to the spirit of music, or possibly to show off his own gifts to advantage. Thus no two performances were alike. The composer knew that his score was not unlike a blueprint from which a performer could work. As you can see he had much in common with the jazz composer.

To have admitted that early musical scores were to some extent blueprints for performers (this appears to be more the case the further back in time we travel) may seem to have weakened the case for such authoritative or definitive texts of early music, but this is far from true. The present-day performer or conductor ought to have the same opportunity for contributing to the 'original' as the composer's contemporaries had. It is impossible to make intelligent interpretation of early works unless a score is available which bears the composer's authority. This is what the branch of musicology I've been discussing in this, and in the previous sections, is all about. A copy several times removed from the composer's autograph is of little use, unless it is all we have left today, in which case we are grateful for it. But each time a copy is made from a copy, mistakes arise, so that the composer's authority becomes progressively weakened. This was nicely summarized by Thomas Morley, an English composer, in his book *A Plain and Easy Introduction to Practical Music* published in 1597. He wrote:

'In copies passing from hand to hand, a small oversight committed by the first writer by the second will be made worse, which will occasion to the third to alter much . . . according as shall seem best to his own judgement, though (God knows) it will be far enough from the meaning of the author; so that errors passing from hand to hand in written copies be easily augmented . . .'

Fig. 37a and b   Drawings by Mendelssohn, 1829.

HOW THE MUSICIAN'S STATUS CHANGED IN THE EARLY NINETEENTH CENTURY

The day after Mendelssohn directed Bach's *St. Matthew Passion* at the Berlin *Singakademie*, Zelter wrote to Goethe informing him that the 'Bach music' had gone well under Mendelssohn's calm direction. Accounts by Fanny Mendelssohn and Eduard Devrient, who both took part, state that it made an immediate impact on the public, and you have read that the second performance under Mendelssohn, and the third, under Zelter, were equally well received. We have seen that such an interest in works of the past was characteristic of the early nineteenth century. But it has not been emphasized yet that the public's admiration of the conductor, its reaction to Mendelssohn personally, was equally characteristic. It is this relationship of musician and audience, the musician's place in society and the crucial change which it underwent in the early nineteenth century that we want to investigate in this section.

We have said in the Introduction that composers such as Bach and Mozart probably thought of themselves as master-craftsmen, providing a skilled service for which there was plenty of demand. In contrast with this, musicians after the end of the eighteenth century ceased considering themselves in this way, nor were they so regarded. The craftsman-musician did not fit in with the early nineteenth-century view at all. The Romantic musician was an *artist*, a creative or an interpretative artist, but in either case potentially a person to be respected for possessing rare ability. Precisely what his standing was depended, of course, on how good he was and on what kind of personality he had. The most gifted musicians were regarded as an élite in society, and given the temperament and ability of Liszt (1811–86) or Wagner (1813–83) the artist was revered as a genius. Before looking more closely at the Romantic artist, however, and the difference between him and the musician of the eighteenth century let us try to establish what the change in status was and to indicate how it occurred.

During the eighteenth century many of the traditional barriers in the German class structure had been weakened, and by the latter half it was no longer impossible to move from poverty and a position of no social influence, to wealth, respectability and considerable influence. We have seen that the fortunes of the Mendelssohn family changed in this way: Moses had arrived poor in Berlin in 1743, but less than half a century later his son, Abraham Mendelssohn, enjoyed a position of financial security and social responsibility. This was movement from the lower class into the growing middle class of people in commerce and the professions, the class which by the early nineteenth century had gained as much influence on society as a whole as the aristocracy used to have. When the musician rose in status he either moved up into the middle class, from the lower class, or was accorded a higher position, in the 'upper' middle class.

Thus accepted, the musician became a new kind of professional, earning his living rather differently from the way in which musicians had done formerly. This became possible only when, at the end of the eighteenth century society, or more accurately that part of it which was not influential – the middle class – gradually began taking over patronage of the arts. Except in the case of opera, patronage had previously been the exclusive preserve either of the Church or of wealthy individuals of the aristocracy. Therefore, when society corporately assumed responsiblity, this marked the end of a tradition in the employment of musicians going back beyond the seventeenth century. Like a wheelwright, for example, who designed and made wheels as required by his master, the musician had composed his music as the occasion demanded and taken part in performing it. This was the kind of employment which, with few exceptions, musicians had experienced up to the closing years of the eighteenth century. Up to this time, the best musicians were employed as 'all-rounders', and had to be able to compose, to play a number of instruments well, and to be prepared to give music lessons. Less capable musicians were fortunate if they could get employed as singers in a church or as players at a court, theatre or pleasure-garden. The status of men like even Bach, Mozart and Haydn, was below the middle of the society in which they worked, despite the fact that they enjoyed considerable professional renown, and the chief musician in any court or aristocratic household was regarded merely as one of the more responsible servants.

The middle class was becoming more and more assertive in the revolutionary closing decades of the eighteenth century. The traditional mode of music patronage *might* have continued had it catered for this new body of opinion, but it did not because private patrons did not feel an obligation to do so. Inevitably, a kind of public patronage developed which did take it into account. The musician was released from his traditional obligation to a single patron, and this allowed him a new degree of freedom to work how and where he wanted to. The middle-class paying public supported him by building large concert halls and, by the beginning of the nineteenth century, by accepting regular concert-going as a natural and civilized thing to do. The public supported the musician when they bought tickets to see him perform at a concert. He was in-directly supported when other musicians performed his work too – not through collecting a Performing Right fee as he does today, but through the sum he received from his publisher, and the greater the number of copies that were sold the stronger his position became to negotiate for better terms on future issues of his work. A vestige of the old mode of music patronage still survived (it does even today) in the form of the commission, in which case a composer would be invited by an individual or a society to write a specific type of work in return for a fee. More often than not though, it was the concert-going public that was supporting the musician, and this tended to encourage him to specialize to a degree which had not been required before and to concentrate on becoming a better composer, or else to devote his time to playing in a professional orchestra. If he were outstandingly capable as a performer he might even follow a career as a concert artist. As far as the general public was concerned it was this kind of artist, the virtuoso, that personified Romanticism in music.

Technical perfection had been very highly prized before the nineteenth century of course. Nevertheless, the musician had usually performed his own compositions. Also, most of the leading per-formers happened to have been the best composers. The development which was so significant in the nineteenth century was that though the virtuoso might or might not have performed his own music, he also acted as an intermediary between the non-playing composer and the public. He became a professional interpreter, or re-creator of other men's music. This is an important point. It is worth dwelling on it for a moment and comparing the position in the eighteenth century with that which came about with the social changes described in the early nineteenth century.

The music of Bach (1685–1750) and Handel (1685–1759) had been admired both by their professional rivals and the public, but it was their prowess as keyboard performers which had the greatest and most immediate public appeal. After his death, when his compositions were known only to a few, Bach's reputation as an organist lived on. Though Handel had been very successful for a time as an opera composer and had established his reputation before he started writing oratorios in the 1730s, he always took the precaution, whenever he performed an oratorio, of advertising in advance that he would himself be playing some organ concertos in the intervals. He was known to be a splendid performer, and by all accounts was a good showman as well. For the first half of their careers both Mozart (1756–91) and Beethoven (1770–1827) were better known to the public as concert pianists than composers, and their reputations were made through playing their own works. But the beautifully written, *musical*, piano works of Mozart and Beethoven, requiring great technical skill to perform as they do, were followed by many poorly written, *facile*, pieces by lesser composers, calculated purely to exhibit the performer's dazzling virtuosity.

The early nineteenth-century fashion-centre of Europe was Paris, and it was to Paris that the piano virtuosos went in the hope of making a name for themselves. Once accepted there, they could profitably embark on extended concert tours. Theirs was fashionable music; written and performed by such as Kalkbrenner (1785–1849), Czerny (1791–1857), Herz (1806–87), Thalberg (1812–71) and Liszt when he was a child prodigy. The many *concert-studies*, *airs with variations*, *pot-pourris* and *fantasias* focussed the public's attention in the 1820s and 1830s on the virtuoso, in the concert hall as well as in the more intimate and sophisticated *salon*. Pianists undoubtedly led the field, but not to the total exclusion of other instrumentalists. The violinist Paganini (1782–1840), had such a reputation that his ability became legendary, and it was rumoured that the Devil had something to do with his extraordinary technique. While solo performers were demonstrating their virtuosity to a much wider public than ever before, the general standard of competence amongst orchestral players was also improving steadily. The success of one of the outstanding compositions of the early nineteenth century illustrates this point well; when Schubert's Ninth Symphony was first tried over in Vienna in 1828, it was said to be too difficult to perform; ten years later, Mendelssohn conducted the first performance in Leipzig.

This improvement in professional instrumental playing came about partly through an insistence on better orchestral discipline and partly because it *had* to, to keep abreast of what composers were demanding in their music. This may be illustrated by tracing the progression from the eighteenth century. Haydn's Symphony No. 104 in D major (composed in 1795 and known as *The London Symphony*) is technically more demanding, and presents more difficulties in rehearsal and performance than the typical orchestral piece of the early eighteenth century. But Beethoven's Ninth Symphony (the 'Choral', 1824), Schubert's Ninth Symphony (1828) and the *Fantastic Symphony* of Berlioz (1832) are considerably more demanding than any of Haydn's symphonies. And later still in the nineteenth century, Wagner's operas (*Tristan and Isolde* of 1865, for instance), and the symphonies of Mahler and Tchaikovsky, make even greater demands on orchestral players.

As the general standard of playing rose it became increasingly difficult for the musician to work as an 'all-rounder', and specialization in performance or in composition became imperative. There were a few musicians whose general ability gained them public recognition amongst the best creative and performing artists. Mendelssohn, for example, Chopin (1810–49) and Liszt (1811–86) were outstanding performers as well as composers who made a substantial contribution to nineteenth-century music. Schumann (1810–56) would have been one too. In fact he damaged his hand when he was a young concert pianist, in attempting to increase his span on a home-made stretching machine – that finished his performing career. But although he had lost this means of expression, he found another. As a music critic he performed a rôle that was to become increasingly influential in society. Writing in the *Neue Zeitschrift für Musik* (*New Journal for Music*), which he edited for almost ten years, and in other journals, he published essays and a large number of reviews of new music and performances. He declared his intention of attempting to raise the public's taste in music. and directed his reviews against what he considered to be the cause of the degraded taste of the 1830s. The main one he identified in the person of the interloping piano virtuoso from Paris, with his variations and fantasias on favourite tunes from grand opera.

The composers of grand opera also came in for sharp criticism, if he considered that their eagerness to get popular applause had led them to lower their artistic standards indecently. Meyerbeer (1791–1864) was probably the most famous composer in Europe on account of his opera *Les Huguenots*, which Schumann saw in Leipzig in 1837. It exemplified, for Schumann, the worst characteristics of the spectacular style of Parisian opera, and its immense success in Germany obviously distressed him, as his review in the *Neue Zeitschrift für Musik* shows.[1] A Protestant could be nothing but revolted at hearing

> 'his most treasured hymn screamed from the stage, (seeing) the bloodiest drama in the history of his religion reduced to the level of a farce at a country fair, all for the sake of money and applause; he is shocked by this opera from the ridiculously vulgar sanctity of the overture to the finale, after which, apparently, we are all to be burned alive immediately. After *Les Huguenots*, what remains to be done on the stage but the actual beheading of criminals and the exhibition of loose women?'

In the previous century the taste fostered by court patronage had been *directly* influenced by the court musicians themselves. Often they used to give music lessons to their employers and, communicating on a personal level, chose the music to be performed. The opinions of the court, the composer's first natural public, were unlikely to be taken into account.

1 An account of the matter, with this translation of the passage from the *Neue Zeitschrift für Musik*, is given in Leon B. Plantinga, *Schumann as Critic*, pp. 160–164, Yale University Press, New Haven and London, 1967.

After the concert-going public had assumed much of the responsibility for music patronage in the early nineteenth century, they certainly did voice their opinions, but by then two-way communication was not as easy as it had been. Although what they wanted may have been obvious to the composer, he could not reply to their demands individually. He therefore resorted to print, to explain or justify why his music, or someone else's, was worthy of attention. Musicians and writers had in any case become much closer during the early nineteenth century, both having become members of the artistic élite. Musicians of Mendelssohn's and Schumann's generation also had a better education and richer cultural experience than the average musician of Mozart and Haydn's time. Schumann, for example, was by no means an isolated case of a well-read musician who could also use language elegantly. They had all read the work of E. T. A. Hoffmann (1776–1822), composer and poet, who is now remembered as one of the writers who had most influence on the course of Romanticism in music in the 1830s. Berlioz (1803–69) contributed to literary journals; so did Liszt and Wagner. Just as the public encouragement of virtuosity and admiration for the performer who was extending the technical limits of piano-playing, in the 1820s and 1830s could be taken as symptomatic of contemporary society's interest in progress, the musician's concern with literature, as with politics and the wider cultural issues in society, was an integral and characteristic part of his outlook as an artist.

FINDING YOUR OWN EVIDENCE

You might wish that you had sources at hand from which you could see for yourself how musicians were treated in the eighteenth and nineteenth centuries. A fair impression could be gained from reading travel books, novels, memoirs, newspaper reports, music criticism in literary journals, composers' letters and diaries. Pictures, too, might afford an insight into life in a particular situation since they can be extremely valuable where written sources are absent. The theme chosen to link the various parts of this unit together is Mendelssohn's performance in 1829 of Bach's *St. Matthew Passion*. Coming back to this then, let us look at two documentary sources relating to these two composers, Mendelssohn and Bach.

SOURCES

Here is a sketch of Bach's career in order that you can gauge more accurately the significance of what the first excerpt contains. It is part of the contract of employment which Bach had at his last appointment.

The pattern of Bach's career was typical of the kind which a professional musician might follow in Germany in the seventeenth and eighteenth centuries. What is interesting is that Bach's ability brought him forward at an early age to some of the more attractive posts in Germany. He was an extraordinarily good organist and harpsichordist and had, in addition to what must have been a masterly technique, the ability to extemporize particularly well. He was also a string player, in fact his first post, at the age of 18, was as a violinist in a Court orchestra. After filling in succession the post of organist at the New Church in the town of Arnstadt, and at St. Blasius' Church in the Imperial Free City of Mühlhausen, he was appointed at the age of 23, Chamber Musician and Court Organist at Weimar. Six years later he was promoted to the post of *Konzertmeister* (equivalent to the position of the modern Orchestral Leader). Shortly afterwards his salary was raised to that of *Kapellmeister* (Director of the Court Orchestra). He continued as Court Organist, but as *Konzertmeister* was also the leading violinist in the orchestra and played a solo part in concertos. Three years later, in 1717, he had a higher court appointment of *Kapellmeister* to the Court of Cöthen. He had reached the top of his profession at the age of 32. Nevertheless, six years later, when the post of *Cantor* or Director of Music, at the Thomasschule, Leipzig, became vacant, Bach competed for it and was appointed.

The main part of his duties was the charge of music in the choir school and the Church of St. Thomas itself. It was one of the most sought-after posts in music in the Lutheran Church, even in the whole of Germany.

This first excerpt consists of six clauses and the final undertaking signed by Bach when he was appointed to the post of Cantor of the Thomasschule, Leipzig. The second excerpt is taken from a letter written by Mendelssohn in 1842, describing the incident which is also depicted in two of the illustrations to this unit.

I

1   That I shall set the boys a shining example of an honest, retiring manner of life, serve the School industriously, and instruct the boys conscientiously;

3   Show to the Honourable and Most Wise Council all proper respect and obedience, and protect and further everywhere as best I may its honour and reputation; likewise if a gentleman of the Council desires the boys for a musical occasion unhesitatingly provide him with the same, but otherwise never permit them to go out of town to funerals or weddings without the previous knowledge and consent of the Burgomaster and Honourable Directors of the School currently in office;

4   Give due obedience to the Honourable Inspectors and Directors of the School in each and every instruction which the same shall issue in the name of the Honourable and Most Wise Council;

7   In order to preserve the good order in the Churches, so arrange the music that it shall not last too long, and shall be of such a nature as not to make an operatic impression, but rather incite the listeners to devotion;

9   Treat the boys in a friendly manner and with caution, but, in case they do not wish to obey, chastise them with moderation or report them to the proper place;

12   Not to go out of town without the permission of the Honourable Burgomaster currently in office;

Now therefore I do hereby undertake and bind myself faithfully to observe all of the said requirements, and on pain of losing my post not to act contrary to them, in witness whereof I have set my hand and seal to this agreement.

Done in Leipzig, May 5th, 1723.

Johann Sebastian Bach

'Prince Albert had asked me to go to him on Saturday at two o'clock, so that I might try his organ before I left England. I found him all alone; and as we were talking away, the Queen came in, also quite alone, in a house dress. She said she was obliged to leave for Claremont in an hour; 'But goodness! how it looks here', she added, when she saw that the wind had littered the whole room, and even the pedals of the organ (which, by the way, made a very pretty feature in the room), with leaves of music from a large portfolio that lay open. As she spoke, she knelt down and began picking up the music; Prince Albert helped, and I too was not idle. Then Prince Albert proceeded to explain the stops to me, and while he was doing it, she said that she would put things straight alone.

But I begged that the Prince would first play me something so that, as I said, I might boast about it in Germany; and thereupon he played me a chorale by heart, with pedals, so charmingly and clearly and correctly that many an organist could have learned something; and the Queen, having finished her work, sat beside him and listened, very pleased. Then I had to play, and I began my chorus from 'St. Paul' (an oratorio by Mendelssohn): 'How lovely are the Messengers!' Before I got to the end of the first verse, they both began to sing. . . .'

DISCUSSION

1 Bach agreed to these conditions and others when he was appointed. It would clearly be to the school's advantage if its Cantor lived up to the requirements of 1, and there may be sound common-sense behind 7 and 9, but the tone is officious and to us today this is irritating. The musician in the eighteenth century could expect nothing else, and clauses 3, 4 and 12 insist categorically that the Cantor should show 'proper respect and obedience' to the authorities 'in each and every instruction'. Though highly respected within the musical profession, Bach was treated by his employers as a servant. The severity with which The Honourable and Most Wise Council exercised its authority did, in fact, cause Bach to enter into some lengthy and unpleasant disputes. He had reached as high as he could go in his profession and yet, this was how he was treated by his employers. His status in the community, however, was certainly higher than that of a servant. He was the only Cantor of the Thomasschule, an august institution, and the distinction of filling such a responsible post placed Bach in the middle class.

2 Mendelssohn, on the other hand was not a servant and the letter shows how he was treated with warm-hearted respect by the Queen and her Consort. He was a frequent visitor to Britain, he came ten times and established himself as a favourite with the British public, who were quite taken by his dignified, friendly and unassuming manner. He was socially acceptable, indeed welcome, at Buckingham Palace as the fêted leader of an artistic élite. Queen Victoria and Prince Albert were not in the practice of performing for *any* musician, but as accomplished musical amateurs responded with admiration to Mendelssohn the superb professional, with whose music they were familiar. Mendelssohn says that the Queen listened to her husband's playing and was 'very pleased' with it. She was proud that he was acquitting himself well in the presence of a professional musician,

playing 'so charmingly and clearly and correctly that many an organist could have learned something'. We might note, incidentally, that there was more musical cultivation in Victorian England among the Court circle and upper classes than today, largely because they themselves learned and performed music. Hence the particular pleasure with which the Queen and Prince Albert entertained Mendelssohn.

(Suggested break)

EXERCISE

After reading the following passages make a note on each of them of the points in my discussion which you think are being illustrated.

1   'On November 6th, Konzertmeister and organist Bach was confined to the County Judge's place of detention for too stubbornly forcing the issue of his dismissal and finally on December 2 was freed from arrest with notice of his unfavourable discharge.'

> (*Excerpt from the Court Secretary's Reports, Court of the Prince of Saxe-Weimar.* 1717)

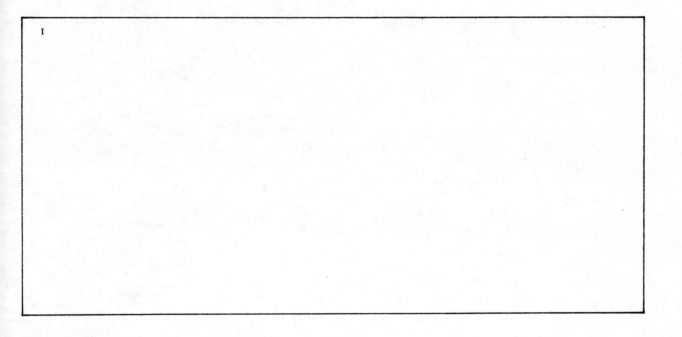

1

2a   'Your Majesty has graciously expressed her keen sympathy in the tragic loss which has just been inflicted upon me. If anything could console me for the cruel sorrow which I have just experienced, it would be the affection shown to me from all quarters, and by Your Majesty and His Royal Highness, Prince Albert.

Unhappily, in such a trial, there is no human consolation. Thanks to the infinite mercy of God, I shall follow alone a path bare of all joy.

In expressing to Your Majesty and to His Royal Highness, Prince Albert, my profoundest gratitude for this kind sympathy,

I remain, your very humble,
Cécile Mendelssohn Bartholdy.'

2b   '*Your Magnificences, Most Noble, Steadfast and Most Learned, as well as Most Wise and Most Highly Esteemed Sirs!*

Whereas it has pleased the inscrutable counsel and will of our otherwise so loving Father in Heaven to take from his earthly life, a few days ago, my dear husband, the Director of Music and Cantor of the Thomasschule here, in blessed death, and thus to leave me in the most sad estate of a widow; and whereas it has for a long time been the custom at the Thomasschule for the widows of deceased Cantors to receive a half-year's grace after the death of their husbands, and such was enjoyed by my predecessor the Widow Kuhnau, and before her by the Widow Schall; now therefore I make bold humbly to address Your Magnificences and You, Most Noble and Most Wise Sirs, with the most obedient prayer that Your Honours will deign, by virtue of Your Honours' inborn condescension and world-famous kindness, most graciously to have the same favour shown to me also; for which I shall strive to be my life long, with all conceivable respect,

Your Magnificences' and, Most Noble, Most Honoured, and Most Wise Sirs, Your most obedient servant,'

Anna Magdalena Bach.
Widow.

Leipzig, August 15th, 1750.

2a and 2b

3   'This was the most expensive concert of the year: no one since Paganini had ventured to place so high a price on the exhibition of his talent as the young and celebrated S. Thalberg. Far be it from us to think of reproaching him for it! On the contrary, we think it honourable and significant: of all the forms of praise we choose the least banal, the least equivocal, and we report that in spite of the 20 francs it cost to hear the great pianist, the crowd pressed and jammed itself into the parlours of Erard: you understand what sort of crowd – the fine flower, the choice aristocracy of dilettantism! It is a real pleasure to raise the tax on art for those who bear it so easily, and with such good grace!'

Revue et gazette musicale, 1838, p. 151.

3

4a   'Fifty and more years ago it was the custom for the organ to remain silent in church on Palm Sunday, and on that day, because it was the beginning of Holy Week, there was no music. But gradually the Passion Story, which had formerly been sung in simple plain chant, humbly and reverently, began to be sung with many kinds of instruments in the most elaborate fashion, occasionally mixing in a little setting of a Passion Chorale which the whole congregation joined in singing, and then the mass of instruments fell to again. When in a large town this Passion music was done for the first time, with twelve violins, many oboes, bassoons, and other instruments, many people were astonished and did not know what to make of it. In the pew of a noble family in church, many Ministers and Noble Ladies were present, who sang the first Passion Chorale out of their books with great devotion. But when this theatrical music began, all these people were thrown into the greatest bewilderment, looked at each other, and said: "What will come of this?" An old widow of the nobility said: "God save us, my children! It's just as if one were at an Opera Comedy." But everyone was genuinely displeased by it and voiced just complaints against it. There are, it is true, some people who take pleasure in such idle things, especially if they are of sanguine temperament and inclined to sensual pleasure. Such persons defend large-scale church compositions as best they may, and hold others to be crotchety and of melancholy temperament – as if they alone possessed the wisdom of Solomon, and others had no understanding.'

    Historical account by Christian Gerber, which appeared in 1732, three years after the first performance of Bach's St. Matthew Passion, *and which probably refers to that work.*

4b   'Never have I felt a holier solemnity vested in a congregation than in the performers and audience that evening.

    Our concert made an extraordinary sensation in the educated circles of Berlin. The resuscitation of the popular effect created by a half-forgotten genius was felt to be of epochal import. A second performance was called for, which took place on the 21st March, and was crowded like the first. There was yet one more, under Zelter, after Felix's departure, on Good Friday, the 17th April, in lieu of the usual *Tod Jesu* [Death of Jesus] by Graun.

    All the musical world of today knows how the sensation made by these performances caused other towns to make similar attempts;

how the other Passions of Bach were taken in hand, especially that according to St. John; how attention was then turned upon the instrumental productions of the old master, how they were published, made into bravura pieces for concert use, etc. The worshippers of Bach, however, must not forget that this new cult of Bach dates from the 11th of March, 1829, and that it was Felix Mendelssohn who gave new vitality to the greatest and most profound of composers.'

Recollections, (1869), of Eduard Devrient, who helped Mendelssohn in the preparations and sang in the performance.

4a and 4b

5   'Lengthily as I have spoken here about the nature of music, in comparison with the other art varieties (a procedure fully justified, I may add, by the peculiar character of music and by the peculiar and truly productive developmental process resulting from this character), I am well aware of the many sided incompleteness of my discussion; not one book, however, but many books would be needed to lay bare exhaustively the immorality, the weakness, the meanness of the ties connecting our modern music and our modern life; to explore the unfortunate over-emotional side of music, which makes it subject to the speculation of our education maniacs, our "improvers of the people," who seek to mix the honey of music with the vinegar – sourish sweat of the mistreated factory worker as the one possible mitigation of his sufferings (somewhat as our sages of the state and bourse are at pains to stuff the servile rags of religion into the gaping holes in the policeman's care of society); and finally to explain the saddening psychological phenomenon that a man may be not only cowardly and base, but also *stupid*, without these qualities preventing him from being a perfectly respectable musician.'

Wagner: *The Art Work of the Future* (1850).

5.

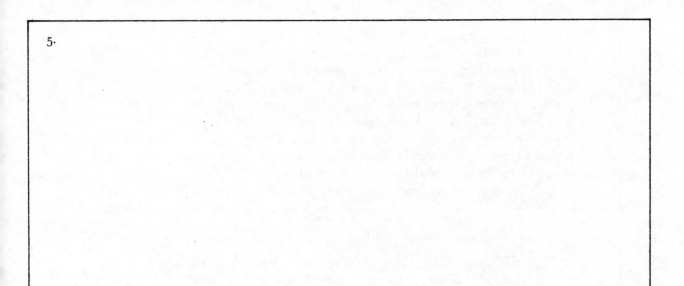

DISCUSSION

Here are the points I think the quotations illustrate. You may have
seen different ones from the points I have noted here and perhaps
I have missed some. But if you have not felt the same general kind
of emphasis as I have, or have not been convinced that there was a
change which was of any significance, I think you ought to read the
quotations again and after that go back over the discussion from the
beginning.

<blockquote>

1   The composer of the *St. Matthew Passion* spent a month in gaol
for being too headstrong. We know he was highly regarded as a
musician at that time, because he held the post of *Konzertmeister*
at *Kapellmeister* salary. The excerpt underlines the fact that he
was, nevertheless, treated like a servant when he had annoyed
his employer, and was committed to prison.

</blockquote>

<blockquote>

2a   The difference between these two letters in tone and content
and   is, I think, particularly striking, and reveals the status that
2b   each of the musicians used to have. Mendelssohn's widow was
writing to acknowledge Queen Victoria's condolences (she also
had letters of sympathy from the kings of Prussia and Saxony),
while only a few days after her husband's death, Bach's
widow was laying claim to rights she feared might be denied
her.

</blockquote>

3   This gives an indication of the piano virtuoso's popularity in Paris during the 1830s. The main point comes in the first sentence: the public were so infatuated with the virtuoso that Thalberg could get a full house at his recital despite the fact that he had fixed the price of admission extraordinarily high. The reviewer refrains from describing the recital with the fashionable superlatives. He leaves the reader to gauge how good it was by stating how much it cost to get in, and subtly hints at his own opinion of the situation by portraying the public as an ill-mannered crowd scrambling to get at the culture.

4a and 4b   That the same music raised a commotion through being considered too theatrical in 1729, and yet instilled the congregation at Mendelssohn's performance with 'holy solemnity' exactly a hundred years later, tells us more about the audience participation than the music itself. The *St. Matthew Passion* is 'theatrical' only in that it is a dramatic work, and that its movements have plenty of variety in kind and colour. I certainly would not accept that it is theatrical in the sense that this church music is really music of the theatre. The early eighteenth-century congregation was shocked at the novelty of hearing music like this in Holy Week, the nineteenth-century audience was impressed because it was so old and dignified. I feel that the account given in 4b, which is biased for what Mendelssohn and Devrient (the person who wrote the account) were said to have achieved, has a ring of Romantic artistic confidence about it. Note also his reference to the 'educated circles' of Berlin in which the concert aroused such enthusiasm.

5   I made a point about *artistic confidence* when referring to 4b. Quotation 5 is a short passage, in translation, of Wagner's confident prose. This remarkable man was regarded, not surprisingly I think, as genius by his contemporaries. He had a greater influence through his music than any other composer in the mid-nineteenth century. He also made his influence felt in wider circles too, through his writings. Philosophizing about music was seldom done in the eighteenth century, never, as far as I am aware, in such a strongly personal, confident manner as in this quotation. In the essay from which it is taken, Wagner examines at length what relevance the modern art of his day had to society. An indication of the breadth of his examination of the subject is given, in this quotation, by two things. First, he states at the beginning that he *has* (previously) spoken about the nature of music in comparison 'with the other art varieties'. Second, his concern with social issues may be seen in his cutting reference to the use of music for 'mistreated factory workers', and religion as the anodyne for the poor.

(Suggested break)

*Fig. 38 Excerpt from Mendelssohn's copy of
Bach's* St. Matthew Passion.

SECTION 6

SOME ASPECTS OF TECHNOLOGICAL DEVELOPMENTS IN MUSIC

In this final section our aim is to make you aware of certain technological developments which have affected music. Some of these are specifically musical, such as the development of instruments and of their organization in the orchestra. We will compare and contrast the sort of performance that Bach would have directed of his *St. Matthew Passion* with the one that Mendelssohn gave on March 11, 1829, in the light of such developments. This in turn leads us on to question the nature of a musical performance and whether, in fact, there is any such thing as a 'definitive' one.

The 'freezing' on disc or tape of a potentially 'definitive' performance brings us at once in touch with modern technology with its advantages and disadvantages. But if it were not for the musical score that readily enables us to compare one recording with another, it is unlikely that we should be preoccupied with the matter at all. So we must examine the nature of oral and written traditions in music. In conclusion we return to our main subject – Felix Mendelssohn and his revival of Bach's *St. Matthew Passion*, summarizing some of the results of this epoch-making event.

You will have two pieces of work to do: a self-marked exercise, and a final tutor-marked assignment relating to the whole block.

Let us begin by considering some of the developments that have taken place in musical instruments. But, first, why should such developments occur at all? There are a variety of interacting reasons. An instrument maker, like any other craftsman, is anxious to develop and improve his product. But he may first need to know what there is about it that the user would wish to alter. It is hardly possible to offer generalizations, because no two types of musical instrument pose the same musical problems, so we will take specific examples.

An instrument with some basic limitation obviously proves frustrating for those who write for it or play it. The early trumpet was such an instrument. This 'natural' instrument possessed a relatively small and delicate tone, which in Bach's day could be used to accompany a solo voice. Unfortunately it was severely restricted in the notes that could be obtained from it. With the invention and addition of valves in the early nineteenth century (around the time of Mendelssohn's revival of the *St. Matthew Passion*) a full chromatic scale could readily be obtained. But the additional mechanism of the valve trumpet altered the tone previously associated with the natural trumpet. Gone forever was the light, singing tone of the instrument Bach knew, and instead it was the heavier, louder, 'fatter' tone of the instrument that Mendelssohn grew up with, similar to that we know today.

Similarly, the natural flute had a purer and sweeter tone than the 'modern' one, whose tone is dampened by the weight of the key mechanism. The advantage of greater range and flexibility must be weighed against the loss of tonal beauty. These developments are generally one-way developments; very seldom is an 'improved' instrument subsequently simplified to produce a purer and more delicate sound. A rare but important exception is the organ, developed to excess in the nineteenth century and restored by some builders to its 'neo-classic' state in the twentieth century. We shall discuss this in more detail shortly.

We have spoken briefly of instruments having some basic limitation being developed or 'improved' to overcome it, with the likelihood of an accompanying change in tone-quality. But what of those which seem satisfactory in their natural state but are nevertheless developed by instrument makers? Most instruments undergo such development at some period or other. They either survive it and emerge in a relatively steady state like the concert piano, which achieved its present form about a hundred years ago, or else it kills them off, as it did the lute and harpsichord. (The subsequent revival of these instruments does not alter this fact, for the revival was a deliberate movement on the part of musicologists to recreate the appropriate sonorities for performances of earlier music – a by-product of *March 11, 1829*.)

It is not easy to pin-point the reasons for this seemingly unnecessary development. We may, perhaps, observe that development and 'progress' is characteristic of Western culture in general. The story related by the Roman theorist Boethius (*c*. 480–524) and others, concerning Timotheus of Miletus, who having added a single string to his cithara and thereby made music more complicated was ordered to snip it off and leave the district, seems amusing to those brought up in Western culture. Yet we may be sure that the above story, whether true or apocryphal enshrined a serious non-Western concept: faith in, and a desire to preserve, the present; and a lack of enthusiasm for the future and for the idea of progress.

Performers, especially the more virtuosic ones, certainly exert additional influence on the development of musical instruments. In order to demonstrate their superior powers, they need to exploit their instruments' potentialities to the full. Audiences have generally encouraged them in this, for the virtuoso is as appealing as the magician in that both can apparently achieve the impossible. Thus the louder, the more flexible, and to some extent the greater in range and size any instrument became, the more delighted the virtuoso performer and his audience would be. There was the attendant danger, of course, that the performer would be tempted to indulge in mere display as opposed to genuine musicianship. There has never been a shortage of composers to provide music for such players, although very often in this situation composer and performer are one.

The more serious-minded composers tend to be somewhat conservative in these matters, being too busy writing music to have much time to devote to persuading instrument makers to modify existing instruments or devise new ones. They are, of course, influenced by genuinely outstanding performers, and there are numerous instances of works which were composed specifically for such men: Mozart's four horn concertos, written for Ignaz Leutgeb (d. 1811) provide one such example.

Occasionally the composer himself exerts the pressure. Wagner (1813–1883), ever exceptional, found time to devise new brass instruments in addition to composing large-scale operas to his own texts and producing a considerable amount of purely literary work. He devised these instruments because he wanted to write eight-part harmony for horns in *The Ring*, his great opera-cycle, and therefore added to his four French horns the following brass instruments: two tenor tubas, two bass tubas, and a double-bass tuba (which doubled the bass tuba an octave lower). These four new instruments, subsequently modified, are known as 'Wagner Tubas'.

There is frequently a definable pattern to the development of musical instruments. The early lute, for example, developed over many years and reached perfection towards the end of the sixteenth century. Then various 'improvements' were made, in particular the addition of further strings. These strings were bass ones of greater length than any of the existing strings, and it was therefore necessary to make the neck of the instrument longer to accommodate them. Furthermore, the increased tension that resulted from these additional strings meant that the instrument had to be made much stronger. Later, even more strings were added, the neck of the instrument was divided into two parts (one for the longer strings and one for the previous five or six strings), and eventually the instrument was no longer the same lute that composers had been writing for. True, performers could now accomplish feats hitherto impossible, but from this time on composers seemed less interested in writing lute music, and despite further 'improved' versions the instrument fell into disuse.

The history of the harpsichord's development is much the same. This instrument achieved its height in the harpsichords made by the Ruckers family in Antwerp in the sixteenth and seventeenth centuries, and in the French instruments of the mid-eighteenth century. When the pianoforte was invented around the beginning of the eighteenth century, some harpsichord makers felt it necessary to 'improve' their instruments in order to compete with the new arrival, which at this time was nothing like so sophisticated an instrument as the harpsichord. (When Bach first saw the early pianos built in the workshops of Silbermann, the famous organ builder, he was not much impressed by them.) Harpsichord makers, in an effort to make their instruments capable of playing *piano e forte*, devised a sort of louvre system of shutters controlled by a pedal – not unlike the swell-box which was developed later on organs. Extra ranks of strings were added, and before long the harpsichord became over-ripe and seedy as the lute had done. The harpsichord, in fact, had been usurped by the piano – an instrument so different from it, that rivalry ought never to have existed between them.

Of all musical instruments, the one that has been most affected by technology since its invention, and since what many regard as its perfection in Bach's day, is the organ. True, many organs were large in Bach's day, having four keyboards, a pedal keyboard, and many stops incorporating thousands of pipes. These organs were blown by hand, or by foot, several men providing the necessary wind-pressure by working a series of bellows. Despite the size of some of these instruments, the wind-pressure was low and this gives the best results. Furthermore, the player had direct contact from his finger when he pressed the key down, through to the mechanism which released the sound into the pipe. He thus had a kind of responsiveness from the instrument found only in this type of mechanism, which is known as 'tracker' action.

In the nineteenth century there was no limit to the amount of air that could be provided by bellows fed by air blown by motors. Furthermore, the organ could be spread over a much wider site, because the player no longer directly controlled the key-to-pipe mechanism. The direct control was replaced by what is known as a tubular-pneumatic action. When the player pressed down a note he allowed air to travel from that note through to the appropriate part of the organ mechanism which then released a valve and made the appropriate pipe speak. There was sometimes a serious time-lag in this mechanism, but that was not considered too important. Later on, electro-pneumatic actions increased the responsiveness of the player's touch. However, neither of these systems compares favourably with the early 'tracker' action, because in neither system does the player have this immediate and real contact between key and pipe. Virtuoso performers of the nineteenth century exploited the tonal capabilities of those huge organs to the full, beguiling audiences with inflated performances of Bach and Handel, and dazzling arrangements of contemporary orchestral music. There was, in fact, a demand for such arrangements of orchestral music, since the radio and gramophone were not yet established. For those who were unable to attend a live concert, perhaps the only chance of hearing favourite orchestral or operatic music was at an organ recital. Composers, in writing for these vast organs, produced a kind of music quite unlike the music written for the organs of Bach's or Handel's day. Unfortunately, organists played Bach and Handel in the same way that they played contemporary compositions, and it is at least arguable that Bach might not have recognized his music in this new guise.

In the second television programme you can see and hear for yourself some organ music by Handel played in an inflated nineteenth-century text on an instrument built in 1904 to nineteenth-century ideals, and then on an instrument which was built in about 1680 and which Handel himself played. You will probably find the contrast quite dramatic.

Although Bach's organ works, often regarded as among his most representative music, were admired by musicians early on in the 'revival', it was not until the second and third decades of this century that musicians experienced a growing desire to hear this music on the kinds of instruments for which he wrote it. A 'neo-classic' style of organ building developed, which once again used low wind-pressures, tracker actions, and the kinds of pipework Bach's contemporaries admired. Some concessions were made to later music and modern technology. At their best, some of these instruments give a new insight into early music, yet are versatile enough to accommodate later music too. In fact, they have stimulated prominent composers to take organ composition seriously again after fifty years or more of neglect, and in recent years a number of major organ works have appeared – a further by-product, perhaps, of *March 11, 1829*.

Not only have individual instruments had a kind of natural cycle of growth during which tonal as well as technical changes have taken place, but the whole symphony orchestra has changed almost beyond recognition, due to a great extent to the availability of new sonorities. Thus the contrast in the actual sound we hear between a twentieth-century work, say Ravel's ballet-score *Daphnis and Chloe* (1909–12) and an orchestral work by Mendelssohn, is not just a matter of style and form. Ravel's orchestration, possible for him because of technical advances in the instruments for which he writes, gives *Daphnis and Chloe* its distinctive and evocative identity. If you have the opportunity, try and listen on the radio or gramophone to a symphony or orchestral work by Mendelssohn and contrast the actual sonorities with those in any orchestral work by Ravel (1875–1937) or Debussy (1862–1918). In these later, so-called 'impressionist' works you will hear a completely new concept of orchestral colour. Because of the fuller ranges of brass and woodwind instruments and harps, and their modern dexterity, Ravel is able to make demands on the players that would have seemed impossible to musicians of Mendelssohn's day. Look at the following two pieces of score. Without actually hearing them at all, try to see how very different they are. Jot down a few of the differences that strike you, and that you would expect to effect the sound you would hear when they were played.

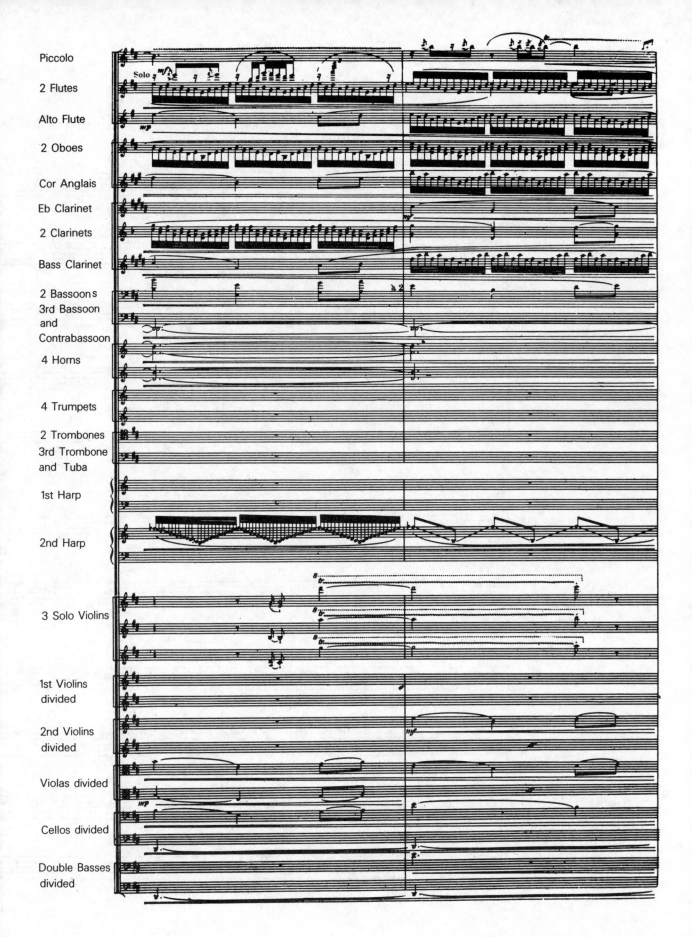

Fig. 39 Excerpt from 'Daphnis and Chloe' by Maurice Ravel (1875-1937).

SYMPHONY, № 4

I

Felix Mendelssohn-Bartholdy, Op. 90
1809-1847

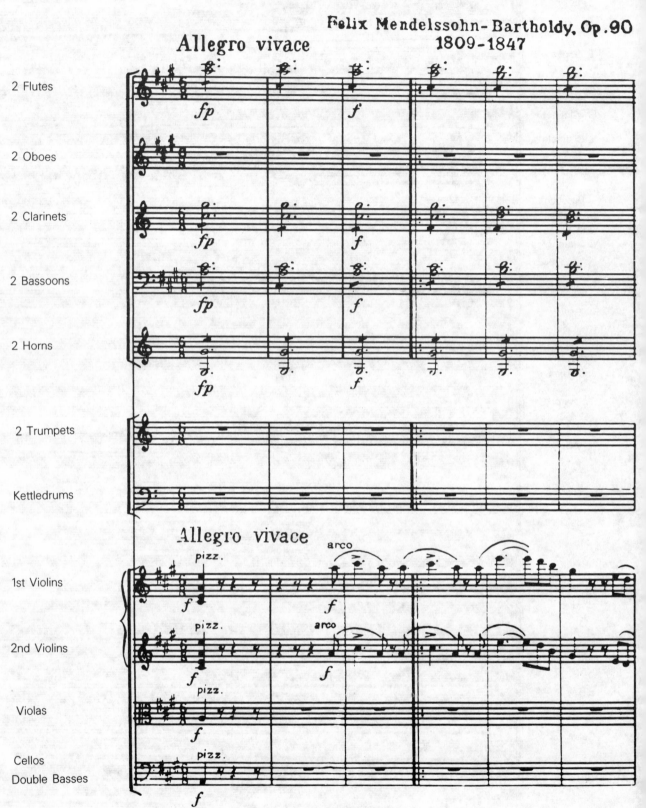

Fig. 40

SPECIMEN ANSWER

Ravel demands a very much larger orchestra than Mendelssohn. Whereas Mendelssohn writes for two flutes, two oboes, two clarinets, two bassoons, two horns, two trumpets, kettledrums and strings; Ravel stipulates four flutes, two oboes and cor anglais, four clarinets, four bassoons, four horns, four trumpets, three trombones, tuba, two harps, and divided strings. It is apparent that Mendelssohn's texture is simpler, also because one can see the tune played by first and second violins (an octave apart) while the accompaniment is provided by repeated chording on flutes, clarinets, bassoons and horns. By looking at the page of Ravel's score one can see brilliant, even virtuosic movement in flutes, oboes, clarinets and harps. It is difficult to pick out which part is predominant or important without hearing it. The solo violins seem to be playing some very curious things.

DISCUSSION

The curious-looking violin notes, by the way, are artificial harmonics, sounding two octaves above the written note. I think it is obvious that the forces for which Ravel writes are much larger, and from the look of the score, more sophisticated. There are many more things happening, and it is indeed difficult to imagine how important motives will emerge in performance. On the other hand it is easy to see that the wind parts of the Mendelssohn are providing supporting harmony, while the interest, the tune, is in the violins.

The symphony orchestra reached its peak in the late nineteenth century, and its over-ripe state in the early twentieth, with many composers writing works for gargantuan forces. Two such pieces were Schoenberg's *Gurre-Lieder* (*Songs of Gurre*), begun in 1900, finished in short score a year later, but not fully orchestrated until 1911, and Stravinsky's *The Rite of Spring* of 1913. It is arguable that the over-ripe period of the symphony orchestra around the beginning of the First World War, led to its decline in the years following. The reasons were partly financial, admittedly: for example, the Diaghilev Ballet Company could no longer afford to commission such large-scale works as Stravinsky's *The Rite of Spring*, and so it either revived old works or commissioned smaller ones instead. Nevertheless, these forced economies coincided with a general change in the climate of musical taste. Composers and audiences no longer seemed to want large-scale works played by large-scale forces. Instead they exhibited an interest in chamber forms. Today (as already mentioned in the *Introduction to Music* block) the symphony orchestra is not unlike a living museum, performing masterpieces of the past and keeping them alive for all to enjoy. Yet composers do not seem particularly interested in writing music for it. Is it possible that after several hundred years the symphony orchestra has reached its maturity, its period of over-ripeness, and its state of decay?

Let us now look at a specific example of the way changes in the orchestra and in orchestral instruments affect musical taste and practice by redirecting our attention to Mendelssohn's revival of Bach's *St. Matthew Passion*. First of all, what do we know about Mendelssohn's performance, beyond the description that Fanny Mendelssohn gave in her letter to Karl Klingemann, already quoted?

The following announcement of it appeared in the *Allgemeine Musikalische Zeitung* of Berlin, dated February 21, 1829:

NOTICE

An important and happy event is before the musical world in general but is especially close to that of Berlin. In the first days of March

The Passion According to St Matthew

by

Johann Sebastian Bach

will be performed under the direction of Herr Felix Mendelssohn-Bartholdy. This greatest and holiest work of the great composer comes out of a retirement by nearly a hundred years as a high festival of Religion and Art.

The Editors.

As we know, the performance took place in the hall at the Berlin *Singakademie*. Among the audience were King and Court, the theologian Schleiermacher, the philosopher Hegel, the poet Heine, Meservius, Head of the Breslau Academy, Rellstrab, the composer and critic, and, of course, Karl Zelter (who wrote to Goethe about it). Fanny's prophecy that 'the Year 1829 will be an epoch-making one in the history of music'[1] was certainly true. Even the immediate influence of the performance was immense. Articles and reviews appeared in many papers,[2] and the following year the score of the *St. Matthew Passion* was published. Clearly, those involved realized the importance of what they had done. The general mood of reception by audience and press was enthusiastic. But just what sort of a performance of Bach's music were they hearing?

According to the German musicologist Alfred Einstein,[3] the *St. Matthew Passion* was 'transplanted to the concert-hall, shortened, mutilated, completely modernized in sound, and – as Zelter expressed it – "rendered practical for the abilities of the performers!"'' Einstein may have been getting his information from the memoirs of the singer Eduard Devrient,[4] who organized the performance with Mendelssohn, as we have already seen.

A recent study by the German Martin Geck[5] gives a very different picture from the usually accepted one. He considers the size of the choir was 158 singers – not 300–400 as originally thought. Furthermore, Geck found Mendelssohn's performing score, now in the Bodleian Library, Oxford. We have also consulted this score while preparing this case study. From pencil markings in Mendelssohn's handwriting we learn about his careful preparation of the score and also what he changed. He omitted eleven arias, four recitatives, and seven chorales, as well as some sections of the Evangelist's part. He added certain performance instructions such as *allegro con fuoco, dolce*

1 In a letter to Klingemann, December 27, 1828, when discussing Felix's plans for the performance.

2 Notably in Adolf Marx's *Berliner Allgemeine Musikalische Zeitung*.

3 Alfred Einstein, *Music in the Romantic Era*, pp. 49–50, W. W. Norton, New York, 1947.

4 Eduard Devrient, *op. cit.*

5 Martin Geck, *Die Wiederentdeckung der Matthäuspassion in 19 Jahrhundert* (Studien zur Musikgeschichte des 19 Jahrhunderts Band 9). 1967 Regensburg: Bossa.

Fig. 41 Recitative from Bach's St. Matthew Passion *as it appears in Mendelssohn's conducting score with his pencil additions.*

92

and *andante* at the beginning of numbers. He added occasional dynamic markings in the instrumental parts. It seems he also altered the instrumentation slightly, reinforcing the chorale- (hymn-) tunes by using flutes, oboes and clarinets. The *Singakademie* did not possess an organ. Mendelssohn directed the performance from the piano.[1]

Geck considers that the performance was a relatively authentic one. The forces involved were moderate – midway between the small group of performers Bach would have used, and the big inflated performances which later became typical of the nineteenth century. The performing indications are not particularly 'Romantic' and could well be followed today. The speed indications are generally brisk and would have left little time for 'Romantic' self-indulgence. But even allowing for this, and admitting that Mendelssohn wished to follow the spirit of Bach's great work as closely as he could, how near would the actual sound of his performance have been to that of Bach's exactly a century earlier?

It so happens that the century separating this from the original performance – 1729 to 1829 – saw major changes in the organization and use of the orchestra and in the instruments of which it was composed. The connection of these changes with changes in taste – though the relationship is very much a chicken-and-egg affair – is defined by the development of Bach's small, chamber-sized group, in which the instruments were largely interchangeable – their 'colour' being used for pointing the different melodic lines in a contrapuntal texture – into a much larger, more powerful 'instrument', the nineteenth-century symphony orchestra. In this, the instruments had to blend into a homogeneous whole, and their 'colour' was used mainly for expressive effects.

The changes we are discussing fall into three categories: first, the disappearance of instruments used by Bach, which Mendelssohn had therefore to replace by completely different instruments; second, changes in instruments used by both Bach and Mendelssohn; and third, changes in the organization of instruments in his orchestra. Let us consider these in turn.

Among the instruments called for by Bach in his score are two members of the oboe family, the oboe d'amore (the alto oboe) and the oboe da caccia (the tenor oboe). Both died out during the eighteenth century, and Mendelssohn had to replace them by different instruments – by clarinets in fact, which must have given a very different effect. In addition, it is possible that in Bach's performance the cellos and basses were assisted by a viola da gamba and/or a violone (the bass and double bass members of the viol family respectively). These were still in use at the time and give a clearer, more penetrating bass than the heavier, expressive tone of the cello and double bass. They would not have been used by Mendelssohn. And, of course, the harpsichord was virtually dead by Mendelssohn's day and was replaced by the piano. Moreover, Mendelssohn's transfer of the *St. Matthew Passion* from church to public concert-hall, another important change in taste, meant that an organ was not available. So Bach's essential combination of sustained organ chords and penetrating harpsichord 'chink' was replaced by the semi-sustained and 'woolly' sound of the piano.

1 Donald Mintz, 'Some aspects of the revival of Bach', *Musical Quarterly*, 40, 1954.

Then, of the instruments remaining for Mendelssohn's use, all had undergone considerable changes since 1729. Thurston Dart's striking comment that 'few concert-goers probably recognize that of all the instruments they hear in Beethoven's Ninth Symphony . . . the only ones whose sounds have not changed since the symphony was first performed in 1824 are the kettledrums, the triangle and the trombone. All the others have been transformed . . .'[1] is applicable, with suitably changed names and dates, to our subject. For example, during the period around 1800, all the strings underwent considerable strengthening in order to produce increased power and brilliance – the seemingly inevitable development which we have noticed affects most instruments sooner or later. About the same time the modern bow emerged. Stronger, heavier and wider than its predecessor, it was a response to the needs of the new 'classical' style and gave greater brillance and power, together with a more singing, 'Romantic' expressiveness. As always, these 'advances' were accompanied by losses: when the old bow became obsolete, its clearer articulation and more delicate nuance, so appropriate to the music of Bach, Handel, and their contemporaries, disappeared forever.

Turning to the woodwind, the century we are considering coincided with the great revolution in their construction. Keys were being added to make extra, chromatic notes playable without the old, complex methods of fingering, which had produced great difficulties of intonation and tone-control. One result was greater fluency, control, and security of intonation (which in turn made possible greater volume). But as we have noted earlier, another result was increased weight and a heavier, stronger, richer tone, with less delicacy of nuance. Both the flutes and the oboes for which Bach wrote (together with the bassoon which possibly doubled the bass line) must have sounded quite different in Mendelssohn's performance from how they would have sounded in 1729. And, if the St. Matthew Passion had included parts for trumpets, as so many works of its period did, then Mendelssohn would have been faced with another change, namely, the very different tone of the valve-trumpet from that of the natural trumpet of Bach's day. Again, we have considered this already when dealing with instrumental developments, but it should not be overlooked in this context. Furthermore, similar changes were occurring in other brass instruments.

Finally, it is only fair to add that while all these instruments changed – and all in the direction of increased power – the *ratio* of a string to a wind instrument, from the point of view of its loudness, did not. So if Mendelssohn had used the same number of different instruments as Bach, the balance of strings to wind would have been reasonably authentic. But he didn't. Bach's two orchestras probably each comprised two flutes, two oboes (the players doubling oboe d'amore and oboe da caccia), two to three first violins, two to three second violins, two violas, two cellos, one bass and one 'continuo' instrument (perhaps also one bassoon and one viola da gamba), a total of around thirty. We don't know the exact size of Mendelssohn's orchestra, but it was made up of a complete amateur orchestra (which, if typical of the time, would in itself be larger than Bach's), augmented by other amateurs and by members of the Royal Band.

1 *The Interpretation of Music*, pp. 33–4.

It seems that Mendelssohn's wind instruments remained twofold (two flutes, two oboes, and so on) so there must have been a considerable increase in the proportion of strings. The change is as obvious as the result. The phenomenon, so familiar to us but foreign to Bach, of an orchestra in which the strings drown the woodwind, is in evidence. It is also possible that other modern developments – such as a higher ratio of low strings to high strings than in Bach's day, and a greater number of first violins than seconds – were also apparent in Mendelssohn's orchestra. And probably he arranged his strings in the usual modern fashion, with first and second violins next to each other for better blending, whereas Bach placed them opposite each other with the bass instruments and continuo between. Bach's method deliberately enhances the contrapuntal interplay of voices in his music, which is also why he had the same number of first violins as second violins.

Bach's two choirs probably numbered together about the same as his two orchestras. Mendelssohn's, on the other hand, amounted to 158, according to Martin Geck, or even 300–400, according to the traditional version. Thus Mendelssohn's choir is at least five times the size of Bach's, possibly ten or twelve times. This increase is in itself an important change, particularly in music which demands maximum clarity of individual parts. But Mendelssohn's orchestra could surely not have been more than two or three times the size of Bach's. We see, therefore, that just as the woodwind become swamped by the strings, so the whole orchestra is in turn swamped by the choir. The trend towards the mass effect, most familiar in this country from performances of Handel, is beginning, and the finer details of Bach's score must have suffered.

It is clear that however hard Mendelssohn had tried to be authentic, his performance would inevitably have differed greatly from Bach's. And this difference is closely connected with a change in musical taste. Did the taste of composers and audiences create a demand for changes in instruments and orchestras? Or did such changes create the possibility of a change in taste? It's impossible to say for sure. Perhaps composers get the instruments they need and audiences the sounds they like; on the other hand composers often tend to use what has already been developed and audiences tend to like what they know. In any case we can say without much doubt that if Mendelssohn's audience had heard Bach's performance of the *St. Matthew Passion*, not only would they have been surprised by it, they would also have disliked it.

At this point we should ask whether, even given original texts and supporting scholarly evidence, it is possible or even totally desirable to endeavour to recreate the original music. Indeed, what is the original music? Is it the idea embodied in the notation, or is it the sound one hears when it is performed? Can there be, or has there ever been, a perfect performance? Does music have any meaning or reason for existing except through the differing interpretations of *various* performances, which are in turn influenced by the society and fashion of their times? Should the living composer (or the dead one by proxy) have the final word about the performance of his work, or does he cease to have authority over it once it is finished? Is his music then taken over by society and realized in terms meaningful to it?

This final question is less relevant to contemporary performances by living composers, since these composers are themselves part of present-day society. We can therefore assume that the style and performance-practices found in their recordings represent present-day procedures. But it is extremely relevant to the performance of music by earlier composers. Should we try to recreate a performance such as Bach himself might have experienced, or should we attempt to recreate a performance which is more meaningful to our own society? If we accept that each generation looks anew at a work of art – and I think art-historians will agree that is so in their field – then perhaps the 'Romantic' view of Bach was as valid as our own. Most musicologists today would say that we should try to perform the *St. Matthew Passion*, for example, in a manner as close as possible to that which Bach might have directed. But is not their view in itself a reflection of current concern with scholarship and authenticity? Is it not possible that the pendulum has swung so far the other way that we are now more concerned with restoring the letter of the past than its spirit?

This may appear to conflict with what we have said in the Musicology section about composers making definitive and authoritative recordings of their music, yet the value of each recording to other musicians and to posterity is hard to over-estimate. One has only to think how valuable it would be to have a recording of Bach himself directing the *St. Matthew Passion*, and Handel directing *Messiah*, to appreciate this point.

Igor Stravinsky (1882–1971) lived through the whole period of transition from nineteenth to twentieth-century musical practices, and had seen also the growth of modern technology and its influence of music and musical fashion. In a book published in 1958 entitled *Conversations with Igor Stravinsky*,[1] Robert Craft asked him, 'Which of your recorded performances do you prefer, which do you consider definitive?' Stravinsky answered as follows:

'I cannot evaluate my records for the reason that I am always too busy with new work to have time to listen to them. However, a composer is not as easily satisfied with recordings of his works as a performer is satisfied for him, in his name, and this is true even when the composer and performer are the same person. The composer fears that errors will become authentic copy, and that one possible performance, one set of variables will be accepted as the only one. First recordings are standard-setting and we are too quickly accustomed to them. But to the composer-conductor the advantage of being able to anticipate the performances of his new works with his own recordings outweighs all complaints. For one thing, the danger of the middle musician is reduced. For another, the time-lag in disseminating new music has been cut from a generation or two to six months or a year. If a work like *Le marteau sans maître* [by the contemporary French composer Pierre Boulez] had been written before the present era of recording it would have reached young musicians outside of the principal cities only years later. As it is this same *Marteau*, considered so difficult to perform a few years ago, is now within the technique of many players, thanks to their being taught by record.

1 Igor Stravinsky and Robert Craft, *Conversations with Igor Stravinsky*, Faber and Faber, London, 1958.

But the public is still too little aware that the word "performance" applied to recording is often extremely euphemistic. Instead of "performing" a piece, the recording artist "breaks it down". He records according to the size (cost) of the orchestra. Thus Haydn's *Farewell Symphony* [a work in which members of the orchestra leave the room in turn until only two violinists remain] would be recorded from beginning to end in order. But *Bolero* [a work by Maurice Ravel in which the orchestra is continuously augmented] would be done backwards so to speak, if it were sectionally divisible. Another problem is that the orchestra is seated according to the acoustical arrangement required by the engineering. This means that the orchestra does not always sound like an orchestra to the orchestra.

I still prefer productions to reproductions. (No photograph matches the colours of the original nor is any phonographed sound the same as live sound; and we know from experience that in five years new processes and equipment will make us despise what we now accept as good enough imitations). But the reproduced repertoire is so much greater than the produced, concerts are no longer any competition at all.'

(Suggested break)

Stravinsky's remarks bring us to the second important way in which technology affects musical practice and taste: how music is disseminated, passed on, and preserved. I am indebted to Dr. Richard Middleton for the following seven paragraphs.

If Bach's score of the *St. Matthew Passion* had been printed, it is probable that such a dramatic event as Mendelssohn's revival of it would have been unnecessary. The work would inevitably have achieved a much wider circulation and popularity than it did. Let us therefore consider the matter of communication in music, noting especially the distinction between oral and written transmission, and also the further method of recorded transmission which may, perhaps, eventually supersede the other two.

The bulk of music created in the world is preserved through oral tradition. That is, a piece or a technique or a style is passed on by word of mouth and the experience of the ear. The extent of its dissemination is thus fixed by the limits of oral transmission. A working oral tradition presupposes a small, stable community – a tribe, a guild, a church or monastery, a village – so that the practice and knowledge of one generation can be passed on to the next. Not surprisingly, therefore, it is associated above all with tribal and folk musics. Equally predictably it tends to preserve rather than change, to encourage continuity rather than originality. Not only is it closely bound up with the nature of the society in which it exists, it also has an important effect on musical practice. Human memory and oral communication are fallible, and human beings, especially musicians, like to exercise their own individual inventiveness and skill. So the phenomenon of individual improvisation on, and recreation of, an orally transmitted, communally familiar and accepted musical framework, is common to all orally preserved musics, from English folksong to African dance music, from Negro blues to the classical music of India.

Notation, as we saw in *Introduction to Music*, was originally an aid to memory. But of its nature it soon usurped the function of memory and ushered in a quite different method of disseminating music, which is characterized by novel effects on musical practice. These effects are at their most typical when *printed* music is involved, and so they gradually grew in importance as the printing of music, which began in the sixteenth century, increased. They are many and complex. A few of the most important are:

(a) The appearance of a professional élite, which could understand and use the notational techniques.

(b) A consequent split between 'serious' (written) and 'popular' (oral) music.

(c) The replacement of stylistic continuity by originality as a prime virtue of musical creation. (For the writing down of music releases the musician from his rôle as memory and gives him scope and encouragement to work out his own ideas.)

(d) The emergence of music history, with its different 'ages', periods, and schools, and eventually its superstructure of libraries, scholars, etc.

(e) A much wider circulation of music, the self-contained, localized centre being replaced by national distribution. This, in turn, is connected with the change from social division by area to stratification by group and class, the association of particular music with a very confined but cohesive community being replaced by its association with a geographically more extended but socially 'narrower' élite.

(f) The appearance of 'national' styles. This is connected with the emergence of the nation-state: the establishment, by printing, of a nationally-acknowledged vernacular, and thus of a national consciousness, and the growth of national administrative and commercial centres, where music was printed, from where it was distributed, and to where composers naturally gravitated.

(g) The growth of a more detached relationship between a composer and his audience, which ceased to be his own local community and became instead 'the public'. The composer no longer knew the members of his audience and tended increasingly to write for them as a commercial venture. The seeds of the modern distrust between composer and audience, which appeared in the nineteenth century, are sown.

(h) The appearance of a new musical creature, the performer, who does not create but interprets, who does not make music from his memory and his own inventiveness but from signs on paper. He increases the size of the gulf between composer and audience by erecting another stage between creation and realization.

From the point of view of effects on musical practice, manuscript notation of music, most associated with the European Middle Ages, may be said to stand midway between oral transmission and printing. Thus an élite appears but it retains relatively good contact with the whole community. The self-contained local centre, usually based on a church or monastery, remains the unit of music-making, for distribution of manuscripts is comparatively small. The split between 'serious' and 'popular' music appears but is slight, since the élite is not yet culturally too distinct. Improvisation on communally familiar material (for example, a plainsong) remains important, and one notable compositional technique is the re-working of a pre-existing piece. And so on. Thus many characteristics of oral culture are preserved in the Middle Ages, when notation is still an aid to memory, as well as becoming a replacement for memory.

It should not be thought that the stages indicated here are historically separate. History does not work that way. It is significant that dissemination of music by manuscript copying retained its importance long after the invention of printing. In fact it remained more important to musicians than printing up to the eighteenth century. Only in the nineteenth and early twentieth centuries has printing taken over completely. Thus improvisation on a bass or a tune was a popular musical technique in the sixteenth centuries, and improvised additions to, or elaborations of, a score were an important part of musical practice right up to the eighteenth century. So too, were conventions of performance and interpretation, often left out of the score and passed on orally. This accounts for the existence of 'schools', connected with particular centres, passing on much of their craft and traditions orally, and leaving only a part on paper. Even as late as the early eighteenth century, Bach was writing his music within the self-contained community of a court or church in a small German state. Orally transmitted conventions, improvisation, communally-used material (the church chorales), a cohesive communal experience – all were important to him. Subsequently the gradual unification of Germany is accurately paralleled by the emergence of a national Austro-German style centred on Vienna. While Bach wrote the *St. Matthew Passion* by hand, its fame being confined to the local area and its life limited by the extent of human memory, Mendelssohn's revival was linked with the printing of the score in 1830. This gave the work national, and eventually international, popularity.

The most interesting aspect of the communication of music today is the fact that to some extent notation seems to be losing its importance. If you have heard anything of the ideas of the communications theorist, Marshall McLuhan, you will probably know that he thinks that the electronic media are replacing the printed word and that their nature is to introduce characteristics of oral cultures. Certainly in music the gramophone record seems to be replacing the written score. It is our musical memory. A good record collection represents the actual musical experience of our society (not a written diagram of this), and it is increasingly the means whereby this experience is passed on, as Stravinsky has observed. Once again music is transmitted through the ear, not the eye. In a way our memory now exists outside ourselves. The method through which the electronic media disseminate music is different from that of printing. A new piece now does not gradually percolate outwards from the centre to the fringes of society, it can be heard more-or-less simultaneously in every part of the world. The composer and his whole (electronically contacted) audience can be brought together. There is the potential here for a new intimacy in the relationship between composer and audience, and perhaps for feedback to the composer typical of musical practice in tribal societies. Trends towards audience-participation, and towards giving the performer a part in the performance, rather than merely telling him what to play, are symptomatic of this. So is the appearance of scores which merely *inspire* or *suggest* what should be played, rather than notating it. The functions of the composer and the performer coalesce, and improvisation (which in general seems to be regaining importance nowadays) returns. An oral tradition naturally grows up around music of this kind, and it is not surprising that performances by the composer and his associates are usually better than those by others. Orally-transmitted conventions and traditions of interpretation arise. One can now attend a performance of a work by, say, the *avant garde* composer, Karlheinz Stockhausen (born 1928), and compare it with what one might call the *archetype* of the piece as it is held in the memory (that is, on the record one possesses). The performance is a particular realization of generally available material, in the spirit of an oral culture. And, of course, completely electronic music eliminates the score, the performer, interpretation, and so on altogether. Not surprisingly national styles have disappeared, to be replaced by an international stylistic umbrella embracing many different, 'local' styles, many of which are associated with local rather than national centres: a university, a broadcasting station, an electronic studio, for example. Style-development and originality, typical of notated music, seem to be of decreasing importance. The decentralized pluralism characteristic of oral situations, in which differences of style coexist rather than succeed each other, seems to be returning, as the confused plethora of styles current today suggests. And in some musical areas the boundaries between 'serious' and 'popular' music, erected by the impact of notation, are being blurred. Mutual influence between *avant garde* music, jazz and pop music is probably only beginning.

Jazz and pop are the prime examples of today's orally-transmitted music, both being in essence non-notated. Pop in particular is disseminated by electronic word of mouth. Both a pop song and a jazz 'standard' exist in a collective memory, and a performance is a recreation and realization of that memory. Consequently if you read through the effects which we attributed to notation you will see that few of them apply at all strongly to pop and jazz. Of course, notation of music has not suddenly stopped, just as oral practices did not end with the invention of printing, and its effects will continue to be of importance for many years, if indeed they ever die. But it is clear that a significant change in musical communications is taking place.

In this correspondence material we have examined a number of matters which can be related, directly or indirectly, to *March 11, 1829*. Having attempted to define Romanticism and to place Mendelssohn's revival of the *St. Matthew Passion* in the historical context (section 2) we then examined the discipline of musicology and its rise in the early nineteenth century (section 3) and discussed closely related subject of source material in music (section 4). In the century between the first performance of the *St. Matthew Passion* and Mendelssohn's revival of it, that is from 1729 to 1829, occurred the crucial change in the status of composers and other artists from that of a 'master-craftsman' to 'creative artist' or even 'genius'. This is examined in section 5. In the final section, under the broad heading of 'technological developments' we have looked at some instances of instrumental development (individual and collective) and have attempted to compare the 1729 and 1829 performance of Bach's music in relation to these changes. We have raised the quasi-philosophical questions of the nature of a musical performance, of whether there can or should be such a phenomenon as a perfect or 'definitive' performance, and whether or not performances in one age of music written in an earlier one, should slavishly attempt to reconstruct the original performance that the composer had in mind. Finally we have discussed communications in music.

We hope this case study has proved interesting and has opened up lines of thought for you that will affect your future response to music. We have tried to avoid burdening you with technical detail, though some, of course has been inevitable. George Bernard Shaw (1856–1950), dramatist and one-time music critic, said that he believed he could make music criticism readable even by the deaf. He could, of course, but we cannot aspire to such heights. Nevertheless, there are aspects of *March 11, 1829*, that are surely of considerable interest to non-musicians, even to those who may have little sympathy for music in any form. The historical aspects, at least, are surely compelling.

In conclusion, we ask you to read the essay *Bach in the Romantic Era* by the distinguished German musicologist Professor Friedrich Blume. In the light of what you have already learnt in this case study, it should not be too formidable, despite its density and the numerous references to people, movements, and music, some of which would be obscure to anyone but a specialist of this period. Professor Blume's essay brings together many of our loose threads, and it has a breadth which provides a fitting conclusion to this case study.

An assignment, which relates in a general way to this *Mendelssohn* block, follows the essay. We think you would be advised to allow a little time to digest this material before attempting it.

If you are not particularly musical, don't worry. As we have just observed, certain aspects of this case study are of social and historical, rather than musical interest. You are free to write your essay on this basis.

BACH IN THE ROMANTIC ERA

BY FRIEDRICH BLUME

The re-emergence of Bach in the Romantic period has long been a familiar fact – so familiar, indeed, that we are no longer fully aware of the unique nature of that event. Historically, it seems a miracle: a musician whose life and works had all but fallen into oblivion appears quite suddenly on the horizon of a new age, almost exactly half a century after his death, acquiring in the ensuing generations a resonance he had not even come close to attaining in his own lifetime, a resonance that gains strength from decade to decade, that has yet to reach its peak after a century and a half and, meanwhile, has engulfed in its waves the whole musical activity of the nineteenth and twentieth centuries. The Bach revival has influenced concert life, performance practice, musical instruction, esthetics, the cultivation of taste; and the effect – 'historically influential,' 'epoch-making' in the truest sense – cannot be fully evaluated even today. What is more, composers, too, willingly submitted to the resurrected 'Father of Harmony': from Haydn and Mozart to Brahms, Bruckner, and Reger, Fauré and Vaughan Williams, Verdi and Dvořák, and then again, up to the present, they have all been permeated with the effects of the Bach legacy, to a greater or lesser degree. The revival of older music, all music-history research, with every one of its results – the publication of old music, the reconstruction of old instruments, and much more besides – may be traced back, in the final analysis, to this 'Bach movement.' Many revivals of other masters have occurred since, but none with such eruptive force, such a direct impact, and such far-reaching consequences. As early as 1827, C. F. Zelter compared it to the Shakespeare and Calderón revivals in the days of Goethe and Schiller.

The historical event itself is exceptionally involved and has not yet been closely investigated.[1] It ran its course amid obstructions and resistance and drew nourishment from the most varied sources. We must not imagine that there was a wave of enthusiasm, let us say, immediately after Bach's works became known once more. We must not imagine that the first printed editions of Bach's works had the effect of stones that, thrown upon still waters, generate slowly spreading circles. Rather, the response to each type of work varied considerably, receptivity was very inconsistent, and appreciation of the works ranged from the most vigorous rejection to fervent enthusiasm. One could, perhaps, describe this unique event as going through successive stages of development; but even that would not be accurate. To understand the Romantic reaction to Bach would, basically, call for an insight into the iridescent, twilight quality of the Romantic spirit itself in its relation to music.

All one can say with certainty is that about 1800 the time must have been ripe, though even this cannot be explained conclusively. To be sure, the tradition had never quite died out; but the thin streams that had flowed on, past Bach's pupils and their disciples, had had no widespread effect. They had trickled away into the restricted circles of specialists; they had set no mill wheels going. But now, about 1800, it was as though a lock gate had been opened: Bach's music poured out in a mighty river, wave upon wave, into the century of Classicism and Romanticism. It caught up men like Zelter in Berlin and Samuel Wesley in London (both of whom still belonged to the Mozart generation), it captivated versatile spirits among the old and the young such as Goethe, J. N. Forkel in Göttingen, H. G. Nägeli in Zurich, E. T. A. Hoffmann, Beethoven, Mendelssohn, and many more. As early as 1800, J. F. Reichardt reports that Haydn is studying Bach's works 'devotedly'; in his old age, Haydn had obtained a manuscript copy of the B minor Mass. Mozart and Beethoven are inconceivable without Bach. A musician so remote in birth and upbringing as Gasparo Spontini performed the *Credo in unum Deum* of the B minor Mass at a charity concert in Berlin, 'as a sign of his veneration.' The tendency gained strength with the full-fledged Romantics. Schumann composed his six fugues on B-A-C-H in 1845. Liszt made an organ arrangement of the introduction and fugue from Cantata No. 21 in 1855; in 1860, he wrote his prelude and fugue on the name of B-A-C-H. Mendelssohn, in *St. Paul* and *Elijah* (1836, 1846), leaned heavily on Bach, as did William Sterndale Bennett in his oratorio *The Women of Samaria* (1867). Gounod heard Bach 'with Mendelssohn's ears' (Haraszti) and gave evidence of a type of Bach appreciation common not only in France with his famous (or notorious) *Ave Maria*. And that is how it went, throughout the nineteenth century. In the twentieth century, Hindemith, Schoenberg, Krenek, and many others have shown that, under quite different stylistic circumstances, the force of the Bach legacy has not diminished but, if anything, grown.

1 The subject has been approached many times, but the veritable jungle represented by the heritage of Bach's music still remains to be penetrated. – Only the most important references will here be mentioned: G. Herz, *J. S. Bach im Zeitalter des Rationalismus und der Frühromantik*, Kassel, 1935; H. Besch, *J. S. Bach. Frömmigkeit und Glaube*, Kassel, 2nd ed. 1950; H. F. Redlich, *Anfänge der Bachpflege in England, 1750–1850*, in *Kongressbericht Lüneburg*, 1950, pp. 131–35; the same, *Anfänge der Bachpflege in England*, in *Bach-Probleme, Festschrift zur deutschen Bachfeier, Leipzig, 1950*, Leipzig, 1951, pp. 44–51; the same, *The Bach Revival in England*, in *Hinrichsen's Musical Yearbook VII*, London, 1952, pp. 287–300; S. Godman, *Bach's Music in England, 1835–1840*, in *Monthly Musical Record*, LXXXIII (1953), 23–29, 69–71; G. Osthoff, *Untersuchungen zur Bach-Auffassung im 19. Jahrhundert*, diss. Cologne, 1953, typewritten; D. Mintz, *Some Aspects of the Revival of Bach*, in *The Musical Quarterly*, XL (1954), 201–21; G. Hahne, *Die Bach-Tradition in Schleswig-Holstein und Dänemark*, Kassel, 1954; G. Feder, *Bachs Werke in ihren Bearbeitungen 1750–1950*, I: *Die Vokalwerke*, diss. Kiel, 1955, typewritten; the same, *Das barocke Wort-Ton-Verhältnis und seine Umgestaltung in den klassizistischen Bach-Bearbeitungen*, in *Kongressbericht Hamburg*, 1956, pp. 95–97; E. C. Krohn, *Bach Renaissance in St. Louis*, in *Missouri Society Bulletin*, Oct. 1955, 25–31; R. Sterndale Bennett, *Three Abridged Versions of Bach's St. Matthew Passion*, in *Music and Letters*, XXXVII (1956), 336–39; H. H. Eggebrecht, *Über Bachs geschichtlichen Ort*, in *Deutsche Vierteljahrsschrift für Literaturwissenschaft und Geistesgeschichte*, XXXI (1957), 527–56; G. von Dadelsen, *R. Schumann und die Musik Bachs*, in *Archiv für Musikwissenschaft*, XIV (1957), 46–59; D. McArdle, *Beethoven and the Bach Family*, in *Music and Letters*, XXXVIII (1957), 353–58; H. Homburg, *L. Spohrs erste Aufführung der Matthäuspassion in Kassel*, in *Musik und Kirche*, XXVIII (1958), 58 (also E. Gutbier in the same journal, XXXIII [1963], 265); B. Stockmann, *Bach im Urteil C. von Winterfelds*, in *Die Musikforschung*, XIII (1960), 417–26; W. Wiora, *Goethes Wort über Bach*, in *H. Albrecht in memoriam*, Kassel, 1962, pp. 179–91; J. Müller-Blattau, *Fr. Rochlitz und die Musikgeschichte*, ibid, pp. 192–99. – Apart from the more general literature regarding the historical approach to music and the 'renaissance' movements of the nineteenth century, there is also a comprehensive body of writings that concerns itself with the survival, recovery, and new editions of individual works by Bach; it ranges from the critical commentaries of the old *Bach-Gesamtausgabe* (1850–1900) to those of the *Neue Bach-Ausgabe* (1950 f.) and includes important source studies, such as those by Max Schneider, Ludwig Landshoff, Friedrich Smend, Georg Schünemann, Hermann Keller, Alfred Dürr, Georg von Dadelsen, Werner Neumann, etc. An aspect of the legacy that is of basic importance to the entire field – that is, the arrangements of Bach's works made in the nineteenth and twentieth centuries – is dealt with extensively in the above-mentioned dissertation by G. Feder, which unhappily still lacks Part II, on the instrumental works.

The grounds for this astonishing course of events must be sought in a complex of very diverse motives – motives that, in turn, partly reflect the many faces of Romanticism. What we call 'Romanticism' (we use the term in the German sense of the word, not in the French sense of 'romantisme') is itself, after all, a very complex phenomenon. The poetic *Schwärmerei* we associate with the names of Jean Paul, Wackenroder, Novalis, or Eichendorff is only one of its aspects. Another is its critical rationalism, its enlightened good sense, still another its classical coolness and smoothness. Its penchant for the mystical and legendary, its pantheistic surrender to Nature, the yearning for 'Gärten, die überm Gestein in dämmernden Lauben verwildern' ('Gardens where shadowy bowers grow wild o'er the stones and the rocks'), the schizophrenic sickliness of the artist, always fleeing from himself and seeking his salvation in the heritage of the past, in established order and certainty – one could lengthen the list at will. As the extant works of Bach gradually made themselves felt once more, they became a mirror of the Romantic age, reflecting each of its many split conflicting images; and the unique unfoldment of the revival cannot be understood unless one keeps in mind an intricate web of continuous interrelationships: in Bach's works, the Romantic age learned to recognize the solidity, the permanence, and the eternal law of music; but the manner in which that age grasped Bach's music piece by piece, tried to understand it, rejected it, altered it, recast it, and finally made it its own affords us a glimpse, in the mirror of Bach, of the familiar traits of Romanticism itself.

The reacquisition of Bach had nothing in common with Moses smiting the rock and obtaining water. It was not a miracle. It was an artificial, laborious, and wearisome endeavour throughout. Pitifully few of Bach's works were known, about the year 1800. The printed editions that had come out during his own lifetime had, after all, contained only a small fraction of his works, mainly for clavier and organ, and they had long been out of print. Several compositions circulated in manuscript copies and were used for didactic purposes. Of the vocal works, only the collection of chorale settings published by C. P. E. Bach in 1784–87, and now (1804) reprinted, was known. As for performances of Bach's works, there were none. Whatever pieces his sons may occasionally have used in connection with their church duties they rearranged into pasticcios. The slender tradition that survived at the Thomasschule in Leipzig rested almost entirely on the motets and on a few movements from the Masses and the Magnificat. That is how it happened that Mozart, on his visit to Leipzig (1789), was able to hear the motet *Singet dem Herrn*, performed by the Thomasschule choir under Cantor Doles; and it is doubtful whether he heard it in its entirety. The *Wohltemperierte Klavier* and some toccatas and fantasias constituted the sum and substance of the music that had made its way to broader circles; to these we may add a couple of organ pieces and, here and there, the *Goldberg Variations* – all in all so little, that one cannot help wondering why the restorative impulse should have concentrated on the works of Bach rather than, say, on those of Handel, Telemann, Hasse, Quantz, or Graun, which were much more widely disseminated and easily understandable. It is at this point that the miracle of toil begins: why, after 1800, did people go to the trouble of digging up Bach's works, which were nearly inaccessible, hard to understand, and even harder to perform; of disseminating them in printed editions, of assimilating them, of training themselves and others to understand them, and of bringing them to life in performance?

The course of events may be gleaned from the early printed

editions. They reveal what aroused interest and what did not; they reveal in what manner Bach was understood. At the top of the list stood the clavier works. The *Wohltemperierte Klavier*, which was in any case quite well known from the manuscript copies, went through a total of twenty-five different editions, up to about 1850. The Inventions and Sinfonias experienced a veritable odyssey of misconceptions. The fourteen books of 'Oeuvres complettes,' published in Vienna from 1800 to 1806, contributed a very mixed assortment of clavier works. But it was not until the 1830s and '40s that the suites and partitas gradually became known. A first small collection of organ chorale preludes made its appearance in Leipzig from 1803 to 1806; the first major collection (forty-four pieces) had as its editor no less a figure than Mendelssohn. He had it published in Leipzig and London simultaneously in 1845, and his corrected manuscript copies, now at Oxford, are evidence of the great care he bestowed on it. The Canonic Variations on *Von Himmel hoch* were first made known about 1835, by a Viennese publisher. A complete edition of all the organ works was not produced until Griepenkerl and Roitzsch, two ardent Romantics of Schumann's circle, edited them in 1844–47. Gradually, a few chamber music works joined the ranks: the sonatas for clavier and violin and the violin solo sonatas appeared in 1804 and 1805, but the cello suites not until 1826. The orchestral works were brought out much later; strangely enough, the first printed edition of the *Brandenburg Concertos* was publised as late as 1850–51.

If the instrumental works were printed in no great hurry, the vocal works were even slower in appearing. The motets were first published in 1802–1803 by Cantor Schicht of the Thomasschule. The Magnificat first came out in 1811, in the E-flat major version. The first cantata to be printed (1821), *Ein' feste Burg*, No. 80, found no buyers. A few vocal works, such as the *Christmas Oratorio*, circulated in manuscript copies. This is all that was known by the world at large, in the beginning. Mendelssohn's revival of the *St. Matthew Passion* (Berlin, 1829) marks a turning point in this field. It awakened interest in the vocal works. In 1830, the *St. Matthew* and *St. John Passions* appeared in print, edited anonymously by the estimable A. B. Marx. It was Marx, again, who brought out in 1830 a collection of six cantatas, which played an important rôle in the history of the Bach movement: the six cantatas remained a unit also in the later *Gesamtausgabe*, where they were numbered 101–106. The years 1833 and 1845 saw the publication of both parts of the B minor Mass. Six additional cantatas appeared in 1840–45; and in 1847, three years before the *Gesamtausgabe* was launched, Carl von Winterfeld brought out three more complete cantatas in his *Der evangelische Kirchengesang*. This completes the catalogue of Bach's vocal compositions published in Germany before 1850.

Other countries understandably took little interest in the publication of the vocal works of Bach. From the 1820s until about 1850, a not inconsiderable number of movements from Bach's motets, chorale settings, and Latin sacred works came out in Austria, England, and France – mostly with quite unrelated textual parodies. In Paris, for example, there appeared in 1856 a collection of no fewer than 371 chorale settings without texts, that is, of use only to organists or students; and as late as 1870, an edition of 152 Bach chorales was published by Gounod, with critical annotations and, again, no texts.

With the exception of the clavier and organ music, then, it was a modest crop, and the selection of the works that were published shows unequivocally what was being sought: Bach the 'Master of Harmony,' that is, of the art of composition, as he had already been considered by Mattheson, Marpurg, and Kirnberger. In January 1801, an article in the *Allgemeine musikalische Zeitung* compared him to Newton and called him the 'law-giver of the true Harmony, which remains valid to the present day.' Even here we see a confluence of two expectations: the enlightened utilitarianism that is one of Romanticism's ingredients looks for a reliable paragon, an infallible authority; and the tendency to take refuge in the established order looks for greatness in the past. Zelter had much the same in mind when, in 1811, he spoke of the B minor Mass as 'the greatest work of art the world has ever seen.' Similarly, Schumann still expressed his admiration (in nearly Hoffmannesque terms) for the 'bold, labyrinthine' element in Bach's polyphony and its 'wondrous intertwining of tones'; when he remarked, in 1838, that he studied Bach for hours on end every day, he was showing his respect for Bach's mastery of form and his desire for sober instruction, very much as Mendelssohn did with the organ works, though, of course, there were other motives as well. Friedrich Rochlitz, Goethe's correspondent and the editor of the *Allgemeine musikalische Zeitung*, speaking of the clavier works about 1820, concluded that Bach's music offered little to the senses and much to the imagination, but only after it had been processed through the mind: 'most of all, he engages the mind.' It was an enlightened rationalism that guided the first steps of the Bach revival, and only about 1826, in the Goethe-Zelter correspondence, does a tone of warm sympathy make its appearance, a harbinger of the enthusiasm that was to follow.

If this rationalism served to promote the revival, the classical coolness and smoothness inherent in Romanticism were to have an inhibiting effect. The element in Goethe's conversations with Sulpice Boisserée that is known as the Pre-Raphaelite spirit in art has its parallel in the theory of 'true church music' and in the restoration movements of Catholicism and Protestantism. Herder, Mastiaux, E. T. A. Hoffmann, Winterfeld, Mendelssohn, and many others supported a 'religious' and 'devout' church music – *a cappella*, quite straightforward in its form, free of excitement, colorless – as they felt it had been in the hands of the 'old masters,' from Palestrina to Pergolesi and Jommelli. Strangely enough, among the latter one also finds Handel, whose oratorios were sung in a very slow tempo and as unemotionally as possible, in order that they might have an 'edifying,' 'devout' effect. It is even stranger, however, that Bach too should now have joined the company of 'old masters,' for his emotionality, his feeling for color, his fervent pathos were least appropriate of all in that context. E. T. A. Hoffmann, whose essay *Alte und neue Kirchenmusik* first appeared in 1814, sensed the misunderstanding when, speaking of the relationship of the older Italians to Bach, he said, 'They are to each other as St. Peter's in Rome is to the Strasbourg cathedral'; but even he did not detect the contradiction.

The relationship of the Nazarene classicism of the Romantics to the reappearance of Bach is highly informative. There were two ways to reconcile the irreconcilable: either to reject Bach because his music ran diametrically counter to the views on 'true church music,' or to smooth him out, polish him, make him devout, Nazarenize him. Both paths were pursued. Even the plain chorale settings by Bach had met with much heated opposition. J. A. P. Schulz had turned against the 'pomp of erudition' already in 1790 and had criticized their 'massed dissonant progressions'; he found fault with Bach's settings because they had no regard 'for that simplicity, which is so necessary to the common man's powers of understanding.' Justus Thibaut, in Heidelberg, showed due admiration for Bach's craftsmanship, but criticized him nevertheless (in 1825): 'he strove rather to bring the art of figural music [i.e., contrapuntal technique] to the highest perfection.' Abbé Vogler published a comparison of Bach's chorale settings with some of his own fashionable efforts as early as 1800, and about 1820 he brought out a very singular *opus perfectum: Zwölf Choräle von J. S. Bach, umgearbeitet von Vogler und zergliedert von Carl Maria von Weber,*[2] who was his pupil. Here one could see the mistakes Bach had made, and how he might have done better from the point of view of 'true church music.' Carl von Winterfeld's peculiar vacillation between unwilling recognition and distant rejection of Bach's sacred music can be traced back to the same views.

That views of this sort did not lead to Bach's quick disappearance all over again may be attributed to Romanticism's antiquarian leanings, to its flight from the present, to its submission to the authority of the history it saw embodied in Bach. Schumann said that he 'daily confessed himself before this sublime man' and that 'through him he endeavoured to cleanse and fortify' himself (1840). But since the deep conflict between the sacred-music requirements of the Nazarenes and the reality of Bach's music could not be argued away, two expedients were resorted to: those of his works that best conformed to the commandments of 'true church music' were pushed into the foreground – namely, the simple chorale settings, the motets, and certain movements from his latin sacred works; or else Bach's vocal works were substantially retouched.

The works that met with the greatest opposition were the ones that had the 'atrocious German sacred texts,' as Zelter called them; that is, the cantatas and the Passions. The recitative-and-aria poems of Neumeister's circle were as unpalatable to the early nineteenth century as were the abundant coloraturas and high pathos of the aria compositions, the furiously active diction of the recitatives, the pictorial riches of the agitated choral movements. Added to this, there was the many-colored, deeply emotional instrumentation, with the unavoidable requirement of the thoroughbass (a requirement that had been successfully dispensed with in the motets and Latin Mass movements, once these had been shaved down to *a cappella* size). None of this lived up to the classicistic ideal of beauty. Everything conflicted with the requirements of 'true church music.' The monumental fantasies on the chorale for choir were perhaps easiest to get along with, and it is significant that the new editions gave preference to the cantatas that contained such movements. Often only these introductory choral movements would be published, and the recitatives and arias omitted. Not a single solo cantata by Bach appeared in print before the publication of the *Gesamtausgabe.* Then why were not the cantatas and Passions put aside altogether? Why did the period insist on reviving *all* of Bach, instead of limiting itself to individual pieces? This, after all, was the procedure in the case of the old Italian masters, who were so highly respected. How can we account for the fact that the Bach renaissance prevailed over the classicistic sense of beauty and Nazarenism in sacred music?

The explanation is that at the very moment when the controversy over Bach's Passions and cantatas began a younger generation entered upon the scene; and this generation – again, for no readily discernible reason – suddenly displayed a spontaneous enthusiasm, an unbounded fervor for Bach's music. It was the generation of men like Mendelssohn, Schumann, Robert Franz, K. H. Bitter, Wilhelm Rust. When one reads of the deliberations between Mendelssohn and the aged Zelter on the eve of the revival of the *St. Matthew Passion,* when one reads the reports put down forty years later in the reminiscences of Eduard Devrient, who sang the Christ,

2   *Twelve Chorales by J. S. Bach, Rewritten by Vogler and Analyzed by Carl Maria von Weber.*

or of Fanny Mendelssohn, one senses a new spirit in the air, a spirit that had not existed before: the bright note of youthful, ardent rapture, the warm tone of deeply stirred emotions. The older generation was quite right when, in the person of H. G. Nägeli, it grumbled that the Berlin and Frankfurt performances had been 'enforced' by a few 'enthusiasts.' The ardor with which Mendelssohn, Devrient, A. B. Marx, and others set to work had overcome the older group's sober, rationalistic conception of Bach; by ignoring the esthetic canons of 'true church music,' it had bypassed the anemic historical approach and won itself 'a new world,' as Devrient put it; 'the antiquated work' had been made 'modern, clear, and vivid again' by Mendelssohn. The comedian and the Jewish youth, said Devrient, had brought the greatest Christian music back to the people. They thought of themselves as prophets. They saw themselves as priests of the sanctuary. The enthusiastic soul of Romanticism had discovered Bach the Romantic. This explains an otherwise nearly incomprehensible remark by Schumann: 'The deeply combinative, poetic, humoristic quality of the newer music has its origins . . . in Bach: Mendelssohn, Chopin, Bennett, Hiller – all the so-called Romantics . . . are musically much closer to Bach than to Mozart' (1840).

Now this enthusiasm had highly practical consequences. One was that the flow of printed editions of Bach's works quickly increased, up to the founding of the Bach-Gesellschaft and the inception of the *Gesamtausgabe*; another was that, beginning with Mendelssohn, all tampering with the substance of Bach's compositions was ruled out and instead, efforts were made to understand the works as they stood. An examination of the score from which Mendelssohn conducted in 1829 reveals that all of his numerous markings were purely technical, bearing on the performance, and that he took pains not to encroach upon Bach's text. He did not prettify the dramatic diction of the recitative in any way, nor did he smooth away the surging expressiveness of the arias. His many arbitrary changes simply made the performance possible, and, for the next hundred years or so, Bach's *St. Matthew Passion* was given in this or a similar fashion, of necessity. But Mendelssohn's score unmistakably reveals the new spirit in action, determined to allow Bach's mighty language to ring out in its true tones. This may also be seen in the scores of thirty-six Bach cantatas collected and arranged by Mendelssohn for performance purposes; like the conductor's score of the Passion, they are preserved at Oxford.

The enlightened criticism, the classicism of 'true church music,' and the historical approach of the Romantic period had capitulated to the original Bach. The Romantic spirit that now prevailed in the Bach movement was later passed on to the second half of the nineteenth century. For, despite the abandon with which the ensuing decades produced arrangements – as exemplified particularly by Robert Franz's highly controversial editions (which, however, were still in use about 1920) – one principle remained inviolable: no matter how much Bach's compositions might be tailored to suit the nineteenth century's technical performance needs, all tampering with the substance of the compositions or of the texts, with the expression or the language of Bach, was henceforth ruled out.

Thus Mendelssohn becomes the pivotal figure in the Romantic appreciation of Bach, and his work marks the historical moment of final adoption. With that adoption, neither the older rationalistic conception nor the historical interest disappeared; but both were surmounted by an enthusiastic devotion that saw in Bach more than the embodiment of eternal laws, saw in him the subtle interpreter and promoter of 'rare states of the soul' (Schumann) and for this reason became faithful to the letter of his works. This truly romantic encounter with Bach left an indelible mark in the history of the Bach revival. The most divergent minds became united in their enthusiasm for Bach, which both furthered and beclouded the appreciation of his music for a long time to come. Wagner and Hauptmann, Macfarren and Gounod, Chrysander and Reger, Spitta and Franz all saw in Bach the romantic master of tonal painting and atmosphere. Admiration for Bach the contrapuntist remained untouched by all this; it had long been taken for granted, finding expression in an extensive body of writings. Musicians who balked at his arias and recitatives nevertheless bowed before the great craftsman. Moritz Hauptmann never stopped criticizing the Evangelist recitatives, the thin texture of the arias with thoroughbass accompaniments, and the complicated part-writing for the chorus. He likened these to creepers (as E. T. A. Hoffmann had done before him) and felt the need 'to emerge now and then from the orchid-greenhouse and go into the garden, where the plants grow in mother earth.' This is an extension of the old, classicistic-Nazarene criticism. Discussing the *Actus tragicus* in a letter to Otto Jahn (1857), Hauptmann wrote that it was all very intense and deeply felt, but that there was 'no organization, no culminating point.' In fact, he compared Bach's usual cantata form to a railway train: the first chorus is the locomotive, pulling a row of recitative-and-aria carriages behind it, and at the end we have the 'chorale-government-mail-coach.' But, for all his classicism, Hauptmann still showed the deepest respect for Bach in his *Erläuterungen zur Kunst der Fuge* (1841).

Hauptmann is only one instance of many musicians and music lovers during the second half of the nineteenth century. Enthusiasm and criticism, admiration for the workmanship and objection to the form go hand in hand, come into frequent conflict, and so give evidence that Bach's music had indeed become a stirring experience. If performance practice often had to bypass the letter of the compositions, if the arguments over the correct mode of execution were endless, in principle, at least, there was general agreement that Bach's works had to be made accessible to the public in their entirety and in the most accurate form possible. Johann Nepomuk Schelble, in Frankfurt, had already voiced this opinion in the 1830s; Schumann, Mendelssohn, Rust, Jahn, and many others followed suit. In England, Henry John Gauntlett had pressed forward vigorously in the same direction soon after 1830. By 1850, the Bach-Gesellschaft could begin its work. Hauptmann, a man with a scrupulous sense of duty and mature judgment, was its first president, and its constitution of 1851 forbade 'all arbitrary changes, omissions, or interpolations.'

On the other hand, unanimity went to pieces over performance practice. Performances of the vocal works greatly increased in number since the 1860s. The concert hall remained the home of the Passions, Masses, and cantatas, just as it had been since 1800. The choruses that performed them were not church choirs but the civic concert societies. After William Sterndale Bennett founded his Bach Society in London (1849) and Wilhelm Rust his Bachverein in Berlin (1853), the number of choirs that dedicated themselves principally to the cultivation of Bach grew enormously; beginning in the 1860s, the Singakademie in Halle, under Robert Franz, became a center for the cultivation of Bach in Germany. Public performances of Bach's organ music became frequent from the 1830s on and following the activity of men like Mendelssohn, Wesley, Gauntlett, Crotch, Schelble, and Hauptmann. There developed a tradition that has continued to this day. Performances of the chamber and orchestral works were less frequent. But here, too, a continuous line may be traced, from the celebrated concert at the Hanover Square Rooms (1837) when Moscheles, Thalberg, and Benedict played a concerto for three claviers, to Mahler's *Suite aus den Orchesterwerken Bachs*, published by Schirmer in New York (1910), to performances of the *Brandenburg Concertos* under Max Reger, Karl Straube, and Wilhelm Furtwängler; and this tradition is still with us today.

With the enormous increase in performances, the dispute over 'correct' performance practices gathered momentum; it was kept alive into the 1920s and '30s and, indeed, has probably not died even now. Should Bach be played and sung as a 'poet-musician' or as a 'master of neutral form'? In the first case (favored mostly by practicing musicians, from Franz to Philipp Wolfrum, from Macfarren to Sir Henry Wood) it was natural that one should try to adapt Bach's tonal language to the listening habits of late Romanticism, to 'cover the bare skeleton' of his scores 'with flesh and blood.' In the second case (favored by the party of the historians and historically minded musicians) there arose a demand for scrupulously exact interpretations: not a note more, not a note less than in Bach's score. The sharp antithesis, however, existed only in theory. In reality, opinions crisscrossed at all points. Musicians such as Joseph Joachim and Eduard Grell were often greater purists than the historians themselves, and historians like Chrysander and Spitta were not such bad musicians as not to realize the need for concessions.

In the field of organ and clavier music, the main issue was the choice of instruments; then, questions of articulation, ornamentation, and the like. In England, most organs had no pedal. The German organs of the nineteenth century were giant orchestras whose 'thick sound-mash' (Karl Straube) disguised Bach's counterpoint beyond recognition. In the clavier music, the need for compromise with the grand piano gave rise to the innumerable arrangements of Bach's clavier works, from Czerny to Busoni. The situation changed only with the reintroduction of the harpsichord and, later, of the clavichord (at the beginning of the twentieth century); and when Wanda Landowska performed on the harpsichord and Ernst von Dohnányi played the same works on the piano at the Kleine Bach-Feste in Eisenach (1907 f.), it was the pianist, not the harpsichordist, who won all the applause. It was a long time before musicians and public got accustomed to the old instruments and strictly authentic texts, and it is significant that the great age of 'Urtext' editions dawned only in the 1930s. Romanticized interpretations and romanticized editions dominated the field through the 1920s and '30s.

The German organ school of the nineteenth century reached a point, with Max Brosig and Heinrich Reimann, where Bach's works were being played in the style of Wagner, with tumultuous orchestral effects, extreme variations in tempo, iridescent registrations, not to mention supplementary harmonies that were used to fill in the textures. Karl Straube, 'father' to a whole generation of German organists, told in 1950 how he himself had started out in that style until about 1910, when he turned more and more to the 'Urtexts'; under the influence of Guilmant, Widor, and Schweitzer, he rediscovered the organ-sound ideal of the Baroque, which he found realized in the Schnitger organ at the Jacobikirche in Hamburg and later in the Praetorius organ reconstructed by Gurlitt and Walcker (1921). Analogous developments took place in the performance of the chamber and orchestra works. Felix Mottl, Max Reger, Arthur Nikisch, Wilhelm Furtwängler, and many others still replaced the harpsichord with a small wind band. They worked with Wagner and Bruckner effects, motivated by the best of intentions: to present Bach in the tonal garb of late Romanticism, in order to make him comprehensible to the listener. A man like Hermann Kretzschmar, historian, Bach expert, and conductor all in one, demanded absolute faithfulness to the sources and the greatest accuracy in the printed editions of Bach's works, while at the same time he considered the greatest freedom and numerous interpolations indispensable for performance. His attitude was shared by Bruno Walter, Sir Thomas Beecham, Siegfried Ochs, Sir Hubert Parry, and countless others.

Among the many controversial issues regarding performance practice almost none caused such heated argument as the question, what to do with the thoroughbass? On the one hand, thoroughbass playing was felt to be old-fashioned; true, it was still tolerated in operatic recitative accompaniments, but it went against the Romantic feeling for sound and was avoided as much as possible. On the other hand, Bach's thoroughbasses were quite different from the classicistic basses of Handel or Jommelli; they required of the player a kind of independent improvisation, a powerful and imaginative support for the recitative and arias, a tonal splendor of their own even in the orchestral or choral movements. The polemical literature is immense. Several conductors, such as Mosewius or Hauptmann, got around the difficulty by performing only the choral movements or the chorales, omitting, for the most part, the inconvenient recitatives and arias. Others (Joachim, for example) let a group of cellos and double basses execute the thoroughbass all by themselves, without chords, 'like solos à la Meyerbeer or Wagner,' as a Berlin critic still testified at the turn of the century; and Hermann Kretzschmar confirmed, at about the same time, that it had been managed in this way ever since the days of A. B. Marx. Not until the twentieth century was it generally realized that an interpretation of the thoroughbass in the spirit of a 'manierlicher Generalbass,'[3] as it was taught by Mattheson and Heinichen, is essential to the performance of any choral or orchestral work of Bach.

Another extremely controversial issue was the question of which instrument to use for the realization of the thoroughbass. The organ had been in common use since the day of Mendelssohn. But most concert halls had no organ. The piano presented a most unsatisfactory alternative. And so, the most debated of all performance practices, the so-called 'additional accompaniment,' was resorted to. This was no novelty, for the technique had been applied, for example, to Handel's oratorios ever since the latter part of the eighteenth century; beginning with the arrangements by Joseph Starzer (1779) and Mozart (1788–90), countless Handel scores were printed, throughout the nineteenth century, in which additional wind parts did the duty of the thoroughbass. Mendelssohn wrote such 'additional scores' in 1828–29, for Berlin productions of *Acis and Galatea* and the *Dettingen Te Deum*. Later, he turned away from this practice and advised, in the score of *Israel in Egypt* published by the Handel Society in London, that works of this kind should be performed with an organ – not as in Germany, where 'wind instruments are added to fill the void.' Still, the custom of using additional accompaniments remained common until the 1920s, in Germany as well as in France and England. A report concerning

3   i.e., a bass-realization that employs *Manieren*, or the stock ornaments of the period – Tr.

the London performance, mentioned earlier, of the concerto for three claviers reads: 'The orchestral accompaniments were re-scored for the occasion by Mr. Moscheles, and the wind instrument parts were entirely by Mr. Moscheles.' In some places the thoroughbass accompaniment was entrusted to a trio composed of two cellos and a double bass, but most often it was a quartet – two clarinets and two bassoons, or the like. In Germany, two or three cellos and one or two double basses were still the general rule at the turn of the century. As recently as 1936, Schering tried to prove that this was an authentic practice of Bach's time. In England the problem was dealt with in similar fashion; in 1891, the *Musical Times* spoke out explicitly in favor of a return to the 'keyboard instrument.'

Let us bear in mind, furthermore, that it was customary to transpose arias and recitatives, to manufacture pasticcios from different works (even Mendelssohn did this once, shortening three cantatas to make one), to attach unrelated parody texts to Bach's compositions, to substitute clarinets, English horns (later, even saxophones) for the obsolete wind instruments of the Baroque, to strengthen the orchestra by the addition of French horns, trombones, or, indeed, tubas (as was done by Felix Mottl and Philipp Wolfrum); and very little remains of the theoretical requirement that the substance be left untouched. Performance practice was not freed of the 'thick sound-mash' until the 1920s, with the increase in historical knowledge and the reintroduction of the old instruments.

The most controversial champion of 'additional accompaniments' and 're-scoring' was Robert Franz. The controversy, which dragged on from the 1860s to about 1920, hinged on his numerous Bach editions, which appeared from 1861 to 1893 and remained in use in many places until about 1920. Franz zealously dedicated the entire second half of his life to the revival of Bach. He explained the motive for his activity in 1876, in clear and dignified terms: 'After all, the future will show that my activities in connection with Bach and Handel were not a personal hobby, but resulted from the compelling circumstances *under* which we find ourselves since we are not able to rise *above* them.' He meant: we are subject to our period's habits and demands concerning sound, and we must reconcile them with those of Bach's time by means of compromise. In an *Open Letter to E. Hanslick* of 1871, he elucidated the principles underlying his arrangements. He had enriched Bach's thin textures with additional parts, had entrusted the realization of the thoroughbass to a small orchestra (mostly a wind ensemble); in this way, he had attempted to fill the 'gaps' in the sound and to interpret the 'mood' of the work. His arrangements are discreet and a far cry from the excesses of Mottl, Reger, and Wolfrum.

Controversial questions of this kind, settled as they were in innumerable ways, had their origins not so much in Bach's works themselves as in the inner conflicts of Romanticism's musical outlook. The rationalistic, historical, classical, and poetical currents inherent in that outlook contended with one another over the correct understanding of the phenomenon that was Bach; and the stratified, many-sided nature of that unique phenomenon appeared to encourage each of those currents.

At bottom, there was some validity in all of these attempts and endeavors; without them, the revival of Bach would never have attained such breadth and momentum, and Bach's works would never have been made familiar to so large a public, though the ways in which this was accomplished may look like historical errors to us. Historians and practicing musicians agreed that compromises were unavoidable; a first-class musician like Liszt and a first-class historian like Ambros subscribed to this opinion. The exaggerated heat of the arguments was due to the intervention of certain 'art-zealots'; the expression is Hanslick's and refers to people like Chrysander and Grell, who once more attempted to fight for extreme purism. The time was not yet ripe for what we now call a 'stylistically faithful' performance practice; it became so only when continuing historical research was joined by the change in musical style represented by such figures as Strauss and Pfitzner on the one hand, Hindemith and Stravinsky on the other; and when to that change was added a renewed taste for the sound of the old instruments. A general need for 'fresh air' in the cultivation of older music made itself felt about 1920: away with arrangements, away with falsifications, away with the despotism of virtuosos, and back to the pure source of the music, as the composer intended it! This did not apply to Bach alone. The countless 'Urtext' editions of old music that have been published since then indicate the tenor of that desire. But the return to historical performance practices was not solely due to historical research; least of all was it an 'unconditional surrender' to history. Had that been so, and were that so today, the Bach movement would have come to a dead end. The proper bounds of the historical approach were already formulated in the clearest terms a hundred years ago, by a very wise man – Otto Jahn:

> The philological, historical view that suffuses the culture of our times demands that the enjoyment of a work of art be founded on historical insight and evaluation, and that the work of art be presented exactly as the artist created it. That this basically just demand, when applied to the reproduction of musical works of art, suffers many restrictions imposed by practical necessity is just as sure as it is doubtful how far the general public, having to adapt itself to the claims of the educated, may be capable of this type of enjoyment. At any rate, it is much to be desired that the tone should not be set by the scholars.

The battle over the revival of Bach has not yet been fought to the end, and the conflicting forces that perpetuated the battle during the Romantic period are still alive today. Otto Jahn's wise remarks are as valid today as they were a century ago.[4]

(*Translated by Piero Weiss*)

---

4 The present sketch is based on a lecture. It obviously does not presume to exhaust the subject in any way but has its origin, rather, in the need for a concise survey of the various motives, aspects, and consequences connected with the Bach movement.

ASSIGNMENT

Write an essay of not more than a thousand words explaining how musicology influences the performance of early music and how technological and social changes may affect the spirit of such a performance.

ACKNOWLEDGEMENTS

Grateful acknowledgement is made to the following sources for material used in these units:

TEXT

Richard Bentley, *My Recollections of Felix Mendelssohn and his Letters to me*, by Eduard Devrient, trans. Natalie Macfarren; W. & R. Chambers, *Tintern Abbey*, by William Wordsworth; J. M. Dent and Sons, *Music in the Romantic Era*, by Alfred Einstein; *The Bach Reader*, ed. Hans T. David and Arthur Mendel; *A Plain and Easy Introduction to Practical Music*, by Thomas Morley, ed. R. Alec Harman; Dennis Dobson, *The Romance of the Mendelssohns*, by Jacque Petitpierre; Dover Publications, Inc., *A General History of Music*, by Charles Burney; Paul Elek, *Mendelssohn's Letters*, trans. G. Selden-Goth; Faber and Faber, *Conversations with Igor Stravinsky*, by Igor Stravinsky and Robert Craft; Ginn and Co., *A Defence of Poetry*, by P. B. Shelley; Hutchinson and Co., *The Interpretation of Music*, by Thurston Dart; Jones and Co., *Discourses*, by Sir Joshua Reynolds; Kegan Paul, *Wagner's Prose Works*, trans. W. Ashton Ellis; Thomas Kelly, *The Castle of Otranto*, by Horace Walpole; John and Paul Knapton, *An Essay on Man*, by Alexander Pope; J. Maclehose, *Nathan the Wise*, by G. E. Lessing; *Memoirs and Proceedings of the Manchester Literary and Philosophical Society* Vol. 106: *The Meaning and the Aims of Musicology*, by H. F. Redlich; Norton and Co. Inc., *Source Readings in Musical History*, ed. Oliver Strunk; Sampson, Low and Co., *The Mendelssohn Family (1729–1847)* by Sebastian Hensel, trans. Carl Klingemann; Schirmer and Co., Musical Quarterly 1954, *Bach in the Romantic Era*, by Friedrich Blume; Smith, Elder and Co., *Life and Writings*, by G. Mazzini; Swan, Sonnenschein & Co., *Selected Letters of Mendelssohn*, ed. W. F. Alexander; Thames and Hudson, *The First European Revolution*, by Norman Hampson; *Romanticism and Revolution*, by J. L. Talmon; Yale University Press, *Schumann as Critic*, by Leon B. Plantinga.

ILLUSTRATIONS

Bärenreiter, Leipzig, Fig. 34 from Mozart's Sonata in D major, for two pianos, K 448, ed. E. F. Schmid; Bildarchiv, Marburg, Figs. 3 and 4; The Bodleian Library, Oxford, Figs. 37a, 37b, 38 and 41; Cambridge University Library, Fig. 27; Cassell & Co. Ltd., Fig. 24 in (ed.) W. Gerstenberg, *Composers' Autographs*, Vol. 1, 1968; Durand et Cie, Paris, Fig. 39 from Ravel's *Daphnis et Chloé*; Ernst Eulenberg Ltd., Fig. 40 from Mendelssohn's Symphony No. 4 in A major, Op. 90; A. G. Hutchinson and Camera Press, Fig. 19; Litolff, Frankfurt, Fig. 35 from Orlando Gibbons: *Prelude*, ed. Louis Köhler; Mansell Collection, Figs. 1, 5–9, 11–15, 18 and 21–3; National Monuments Record of Scotland, Figs. 16 and 17; Nationalgalerie, Berlin, Fig. 2; Pendlebury Music Library, Cambridge, Fig. 29; Peters, Leipzig, Fig. 33 from Chopin: *Polonaise in A major, Op. 40 No. 1*, Hermann Scholtz; Schirmer, New York, Fig. 32 from Chopin: *Polonaise in A major, Op. 40 No. 1*, ed. Rafael Joseffy; The Trustees of the British Museum, Figs. 25 and 31; Science Museum, London, Fig. 10; Stainer & Bell Ltd., Fig. 36, from Orlando Gibbons: *Musica Britannica XX*, ed. Gerald Hendrie; Walter Steinkopf, Fig. 2; Stiftsbibliothek, St. Gallen, Fig. 26; Weidenfeld and Nicholson, Fig. 20, in E. J. Hobsbawm, *The Age of Revolution, 1789–1848*.

Notes

Notes

Notes

Notes

FOUNDATION COURSE UNITS